INNOVATION THAT FITS

INNOVATION THAT FITS

Moving Beyond the Fads to Choose the RIGHT Innovation Strategy for Your Business

Michael D. Lord, Ph.D.
J. Donald deBethizy, Ph.D.
Jeffrey D. Wager, M.D.

PEARSON PRENTICE HALL
AN IMPRINT OF PEARSON EDUCATION
Upper Saddle River, NJ • Boston • Indianapolis • San Francisco
New York • Toronto • Montreal • London • Munich • Paris • Madrid
Capetown • Sydney • Tokyo • Singapore • Mexico City
www.ft-ph.com

Library of Congress Number: 2004113118

Vice President and Editor-in-Chief: Tim Moore
Acquisitions Editor: Paula Sinnott
Editorial Assistant: Richard Winkler
Development Editor: Russ Hall
Marketing Manager: Martin Litkowski
International Marketing Manager: Tim Galligan
Cover Designer: Chuti Prasertsith
Managing Editor: Gina Kanouse
Senior Project Editor: Sarah Kearns
Copy Editor: Sheri Cain
Indexer: Lisa Stumpf
Compositor: Interactive Composition Corporation
Manufacturing Buyer: Dan Uhrig

© 2005 by Pearson Education, Inc.
Publishing as Prentice Hall
Upper Saddle River, New Jersey 07458

First Printing: February 2005

ISBN 0-13-143820-4

Pearson Education LTD.
Pearson Education Australia PTY, Limited.
Pearson Education Singapore, Pte. Ltd.
Pearson Education North Asia, Ltd.
Pearson Education Canada, Ltd.
Pearson Educatión de Mexico, S.A. de C.V.
Pearson Education—Japan
Pearson Education Malaysia, Pte. Ltd.

To my family, especially my hard-working and loving parents.
—MDL

To my wife, Cindy, and my children, Heather and Zac.
—JDdeB

To Mai, whose unwavering love, faith, and courage have always been a source of deep inspiration to me.
—JDW

Table of Contents

Acknowledgments

Special acknowledgment to my family, colleagues, and friends, who have had to alternately endure my manic expressions and discussions of ideas and then my moody periods of seclusion and writing.
—MDL

I would like to acknowledge the roles of three key people in my career: Dr. Joseph Street, who provided rigorous training in science to form a solid foundation; Dr. Gary Burger, who taught me that management is an important profession; and Dr. Carl Ehman, who showed me the value of transforming science into business. Finally, I would like to acknowledge my co-authors, who have provided valuable insights and influenced my thinking on many levels.
—JDdeB

Special acknowledgments to the entire team at CPP Advisors, whose hard work and commitment to a shared vision have made this book possible, and to my co-authors, who have repeatedly proven the power of teamwork.

—JDW

About the Authors

Michael D. Lord is Director of the Flow Institute and Associate Professor of Strategy and International Business at Wake Forest University, where he teaches strategy and entrepreneurship in the full-time and executive MBA programs at the Babcock Graduate School of Management. Dr. Lord's research and consulting work focuses on new venture creation, high-tech acquisitions and spin-outs, and global venturing. His work on innovation has been featured in a variety of academic and practitioner outlets, including the *Harvard Business Review*, and he serves as an advisor on innovation strategy to a diverse group of companies, both large and small. Dr. Lord holds a BA with Honors from Harvard University, an MBA from Baylor University, and a Ph.D. in strategic management from the University of North Carolina at Chapel Hill.

J. Donald deBethizy is founder, president, and chief executive officer of Targacept, Inc. Using new computational drug discovery technologies and focusing on novel biological targets, Targacept is developing therapies for numerous central nervous system disorders such as ADHD, Alzheimer's, anxiety, depression, and pain. Targacept was spun out of R.J. Reynolds Tobacco in 2000, raising record levels of first- and second-round venture financing along the way. Before becoming an entrepreneur, Dr. deBethizy served in the corporate world as vice president of product evaluation and R&D for RJR. For his leadership in founding Targacept, Ernst & Young recognized Dr. deBethizy as an "Emerging Entrepreneur of the Year" in 2002. He holds a Ph.D. and an MS in toxicology from Utah State University and a BS in biology from the University of Maryland.

Jeffrey D. Wager is founder and managing member of CPP Advisors, an innovation-focused advisory and consulting firm. CPP structures and facilitates strategic transactions to support clients' innovation commercialization needs, including venture investments, licensing deals, partnerships, M&A, and spinouts. Dr. Wager's advisory and consulting practice focuses on the life sciences and spans the U.S., Europe, and Japan. Previously, he led due diligence and investment management activities for leading venture firms in the U.S. and Japan. Dr. Wager continues to serve as an advisor or board member for many of the organizations he has advised or helped found. He holds an M.D. from Rush University, an MBA from the University of Chicago, and a BS in biology from the University of Illinois.

1

MAKING SENSE OF INNOVATION FADS AND FASHIONS

"Innovate or die!"
—Various

Innovate and die. In evolutionary terms, that's usually what happens. Most mutations fail. Few truly new things survive, and even fewer of them thrive. This is just as true in the business world as it is in biology. The record of various innovation fads and fashions during the past few years certainly is consistent with this harsh fact.

For much of the past decade, however, management gurus, media, and markets preached a different doctrine. It was a "cult of innovation at all costs," an unquestioning, single-minded belief in the power of innovation above all else.[1] The risks of innovation seemed passé.

The need for novelty took precedence. The *real* risk was *not* to innovate. Managers became mesmerized by the passionate but also threatening mantra of "Innovate or die!" Survival was a compelling enough reason to take heed of their urgent call to action. But beyond simple survival, the innovation enthusiasts promised much more.

It was a New Economy. The Old Rules did not apply. To the quick and bold pioneers of innovation would go faster and more fabulous riches than anything the traditional, tired ways of doing business could offer.

Innovation Excitement, Then Disillusionment

Swayed by this powerful mix of fear and fortune, many executives and entrepreneurs frantically rushed to innovate almost literally at any cost. A great number of companies seriously stumbled or even outright failed in the process. Their big, rushed bets on raw technologies and unproven business models did not pay off. Victims of this innovation obsession included enormous, globe-spanning, blue-chip corporations and new technology startups alike.

It's difficult to overstate how powerful and pervasive the innovation mania was during this time. It's useful to briefly reflect and recall the prevailing spirit. Something more than a bit of infectious zeal was going around. In retrospect, it all seems a bit surreal or unreal, even though we all experienced and participated in it just a short time ago. What were we thinking? How could all this possibly have happened? For many investors and employees, much of it probably does seem like a bad dream. In each case, the new theories and new models for innovation promised much, yet disappointed— or even worse.

The World's Most Innovative Company

Remember, for example, when Enron was *the* innovation exemplar, the exalted leader of a new breed of corporate innovator? From 1996 through 2001, *Fortune* magazine had proclaimed Enron the "Most Innovative" company among all its Fortune 500 peers. Each year, Enron placed far ahead of even hi-tech powerhouses such as Intel, Microsoft, and Cisco Systems. *Fortune* explained, "If any Old World company could thrive in the Internet era, it's this one."

Enron was also featured as the new model for corporate innovation in innumerable consultants' how-to books, academics' business-school case studies, and business-media cover stories. Enron was an old-line company that had become a master of corporate transformation and radical innovation. It was "leading the revolution." Management gurus noted Enron's "almost magical mix of entrepreneurship inside with the ability to leverage enormous scale and discipline to get things done." It was successfully pioneering new ventures and entirely new industries, from energy trading to broadband to weather derivatives. In just a few short years, Enron soared from a sleepy gas-pipeline company to one of the largest companies in the world, with a play on almost every new business imaginable. One book published in 2001 boasted that, "[T]he Enron model was New Economy before the New Economy got started."

How did Enron manage to innovate so much so quickly and successfully? Its internal "wars for talent" and powerful rewards and incentives (e.g., generous awarding of phantom stock and options to new venture leaders) fueled creativity and ignited its high-octane brainpower. These novel human resource practices let it attract and retain top innovative talent for the most promising new ventures. Enron's liberating organizational structures (e.g., autonomous corporate venturing units, novel partnerships and alliance structures, carve-outs and spinouts) also were featured as another key innovation enabler. These nimble and flexible structures freed new ventures from the corporate bureaucracy, giving them unprecedented entrepreneurialism. Likewise, Enron's cutting-edge financing, valuation, and risk management techniques (e.g., "real-options" approaches and "mark-to-market" accounting) were featured as powerful leverage for innovation. This sophisticated financial engineering let Enron more aggressively fund and better value and vet new ventures. All these tools and tactics were featured as templates for other would-be corporate innovators to follow—or else be left behind.

Of course, in retrospect, all these factors were subsequently cited as precisely the key contributors to Enron's rapid collapse and massive bankruptcy. Enron was innovation out of control. Any accounting gimmicks were little more than a sideshow to cover up the true underlying problem—its failed innovation strategies, structures, and processes.[2]

Not-So-Disruptive Technologies

The startup world offered other innumerable examples of innovation mania. Few paused to doubt that the Internet was a pervasive "disruptive technology." The web changed all the rules and threatened to transform and disrupt almost every aspect of commerce. But the imminent threats to incumbent retailers looked like fantastic and certain opportunities for e-commerce upstarts.

Online grocer Webvan was one of the best-funded and best-staffed new business ventures in history, for example, and was equipped with all the latest and greatest technology. Its management and technical talent came from some of the biggest and best global information-technology companies. It was funded and advised by some of the most successful venture capitalists (VCs). Even after burning through $1 billion in capital, however, Webvan still could not figure out how to deliver a gallon of milk to customers' doorsteps efficiently, effectively, and profitably. Webvan went bankrupt and liquidated just two years after its founding. The number of other failed e-commerce ventures, some of them also spectacular flameouts in their own right (from eToys to Pets.com), is too long to list. Disruption came not to the incumbents, but to the upstarts.

Incubating Half-Baked Ideas

The explosion of the much-heralded *incubator* concept was another cause and symptom of the innovation craze. Incubators were neither typical corporate innovators, nor typical startups, nor were they simply financial investment vehicles like a venture capital fund. Instead, the incubators were a unique, New Economy hybrid designed to offer both the scale and scope advantages of a larger parent company along with the best nimble, flexible, and entrepreneurial features that startups had to offer. The incubators were a new organizational form made especially for the Innovation Age.

Incubators typically offered their *incubees* a wide variety of different types of service and support (for example, office space, lab space, IT resources, internal consulting, and other types of shared services). Moreover, by being part of a larger parent that could raise capital and trade as a publicly held company (something a fresh young startup could never do on its own), each of the incubees could get more ready access to preferential funding and, thus, a powerful financial head start. The concept of the incubator was to be an innovation enhancer—bettering the odds of success—as well as an innovation accelerator—powering ideas to market faster in an era in which speed mattered most.

Idealab, CMGI, ICG, and U.S. Technologies were among some of the better-known incubator names. They raised billions in capital because the concept just seemed to make perfect common sense. Combine the best of big and small: public company and startup. Provide seed capital and follow-on funding. Share services, support, and expertise among the incubees and thereby realize powerful synergies.

The Economist succinctly captured the tremendous allure of the incubator model:

> The very notion of a business incubator is intoxicating. Just imagine a floor or two of buzzing proto-companies, bursting with potential, sharing space, services, and ideas under the tutelage of well-connected industry experts. The time, too, is right: an explosion of Internet startups needing help meets a chronic office-space shortage. No wonder the past year has seen the launch of more than 300 Internet incubators, two-thirds of them in America—a rate of six a week.[3]

Despite its compelling intuitive appeal, in practice, the concept did not work so well. The ambitious and newfangled incubator model seemed to offer little advantage over the more well-established and well-defined venture-capital approach. What's more, the complexities of the incubator concept—being neither pure investment vehicle, pure startup, nor a real operating company—brought into play all sorts of heightened costs and tensions. Complicated legal, financial, and organizational issues soon followed. Rather than being advantaged, member startups became crippled by their incubator affiliations. Lawsuits from investors alleged conflicts of interest or worse (e.g., Idealab, U.S. Technologies). Numerous incubators went bankrupt or simply closed up shop.

Remnants of the grand incubator concept survived, but in much less ambitious forms. Non-profit and university incubators continued, and even increased, their modest operations. But most of the for-profit incubators survived only by morphing into more traditional VC firms and much simplified financial-holding companies, or by trying to morph into workable businesses that offered basic office space and services to startups.

Reconsidering Innovations in Innovation

In the morning-after retrospective, as everyone sobered and surveyed the post-innovation wreckage around them, the mantra of "Innovate or die!" seemed a worn and unwelcome cliché. At business conferences and board meetings, innovation—at least anything beyond incremental change—became a hushed topic. Instead, it was back to the real business of business: retrenching and restructuring, focus and efficiency, watching cash and waiting for clear signals from the marketplace. The deliberative, suit-and-tie Organization Man was back in vogue. The frenetic and disheveled Silicon Valley dream merchant was disdainfully out of style.

Of course, the innovation enthusiasts had been at least partly right with their cry of "Innovate or die!" Especially in fast and dramatically changing business environments, failure to adapt definitely might threaten a company's continued success or even survival. But these one-sided cries ignored the other half of the delicately balanced innovation equation. Both "innovate and die" and "innovate or die" are very real risks. Deftly managing this precarious balance is critical. This is the key dilemma—and the core challenge—of innovation.

The Rise of the Innovation Industry

Innovation is a gamble. It offers potentially huge rewards, but concomitantly high risks. It increasingly requires big, up-front, largely irreversible investments in the uncertain hopes of distant returns. It involves hard-to-corral creativity, beyond-our-control serendipity, more than a few diversions, leaps of faith, and outright mistakes on the road from conception to commercialization. Companies big and small find themselves struggling with the myriad strategic, organizational, and financial challenges of innovation.

In response to these challenges, an entire innovation industry bloomed in recent years. Many different players promised and promoted their own solutions for the dilemmas of innovation. Depending upon whom you were to believe, your problems could be successfully tackled if only you understood and applied the current, novel "best practice." Such simple appeals made for clear and emphatic marketing messages, if not deeper understanding. Cure-all and one-size-fits-all solutions proliferated.

The innovation industry peaked as New Economy enthusiasm grew to fantastic heights. Likewise, each innovation fad and fashion deflated along with the rest of the technology and market bubble. There is danger in these deflated expectations, however. Because managers are now understandably quite cynical after hearing far too much innovation hype for far too long, the danger is that an entire field of potentially valuable and practically useful ideas lies fallow.

Innovations in Innovation

In our exploration of the innovation landscape, we focus less attention on those unstructured ideas that made pithy promises of supercharged creativity or profligate novelty. Whatever one thinks of these ideas and their promoters, they are difficult to analyze and critique because they offer anecdotes and affirmation more than balanced evidence and actionable recommendations. Instead, we focus on the more structured ideas that promised to power innovation to fruition, all the way from initial conception through full commercialization.

These innovative ideas include a large number and wide variety of different strategies and tactics. In this book, however, we focus on the most prevalent and important *innovations in innovation*. These strategic tools and organizational tactics include the following:

- Corporate venturing, including corporate venture capital
- Patenting and intellectual property licensing (asset-lite innovation)

- Innovation by alliance
- Innovation by acquisition
- Spinouts and spin-ins (spinnovation)

As with all fads and fashions, something at the core of each of these "innovations in innovation" proved irresistibly appealing. As each of the latest and greatest innovation ideas splashed onto the scene, it was all too easy to get caught up in the excitement—whether it was to fund corporate venturing, aggressively patent or partner, to binge on acquisitions, or spin a spinout (see Figure 1-1). The market for

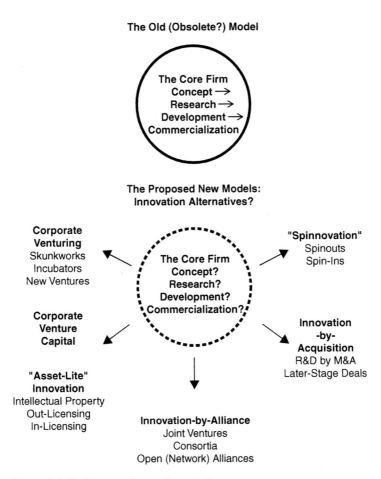

Figure 1-1 Seeking new innovation solutions.

management ideas is surely even less reasoned and objective than the fickle and gyrating financial markets themselves. As managers raced to adopt each new innovative idea that came in turn, the results most often were disappointing and disillusioning. In the aftermath, each idea lost its glow and the appeal of all the supposed innovations in innovation waned.

Each of these approaches promised not abstractions, but rather more practical, tangible paths from invention to market: roadmaps for creating and capturing the value from innovation. Each approach offered a simple and appealing alternative model for innovation rather than a more complex menu of critical decisions and choices. In each case, one or two leading organizations were usually offered as exemplars for other companies to follow and imitate. Many managers did follow these examples and guidelines, often quite enthusiastically.

Bringing Silicon Valley Inside

With the rise of innovation enthusiasm, for example, corporate venturing quickly became an unqualified imperative. If your sclerotic, ossified Fortune 500 company were to have any hope of competing with young and aggressive entrepreneurial upstarts, corporate venturing was the answer. The idea was simple: Bring the youthful vigor of Silicon Valley inside your staid corporate bureaucracy—internalize the same excitement and energy, imagination and intellect, and motivation and incentives. Harness the power and principles of venture capital, the creative promise and possibilities of java-fueled skunkworks and incubators, and all the rest and best that intrapreneurship had to offer.

The goal was to stimulate the underutilized brainpower and capture the latent entrepreneurial energy of corporate employees who alternately had become too comfortable with, or too frustrated by, the old corporate bureaucracy and routines. Become a corporate venture capitalist, both figuratively and literally! Create autonomy and motivational rewards and set employees loose. Let them plant a bunch of real innovation options and watch as they grow. Then, prune the underperformers and nourish the healthy ones—just as in the hothouse, Darwinian world of venture capital–fueled entrepreneurship.

Many corporate venturing promoters went beyond recommending such simple intrapreneurship. They advocated stretching beyond the firm's own organizational and financial boundaries. Don't just act like a venture capitalist, literally *be* a venture capitalist. Use corporate cash to bankroll your own venture fund.

Especially by the late 1990s, more corporate executives began asking themselves, "Why should the Sand Hill Road VCs get all the glory and all the gains?" Instead, let's ourselves cast a wide net both inside and outside the company to capture new ideas with great strategic and financial promise—from whatever the source. Not Invented Here (NIH) became an asset, not a quandary. Let's fund them all, whether from inside or out, and manage the portfolio as would any sharp venture capitalist.

That was the theory, anyway. After a brief but intense splurge on such venture activities, even many of the more celebrated corporate venturing efforts were sharply curtailed or simply shut down after various dysfunctions, disappointments, and red ink ensued. Corporate venturing did not fulfill its promise; the venture imperative became the venture illusion. Even exemplars such as Lucent and Procter & Gamble either curbed or shut down their skunkworks and shut down or sold off most or all of their venture portfolios. The initial, uncritical enthusiasm for corporate venturing ignored the crucial fact that an established operating company is not—and probably should not try to be—either a venture capital firm or a *de novo* startup. It also became clear that successfully implementing corporate venturing activities requires careful balancing of numerous internal tensions and conflicts that venture capitalists and stand-alone startups simply do not have to deal with.

The mixed results of these corporate venturing experiments do not mean that there are no useful lessons for established companies to learn from the world of venture capital and startups. But whatever lessons might be gleaned from the VC mindset and a more general entrepreneurial perspective, successful and established operating companies must not abandon their strengths and, chasing after a dream, try to be something they are not designed for and can never be. Aggressive skunkworks and incubators often are not the right approaches for most companies; they do not offer innovation salvation and, in fact, tend to bring a host of new and serious challenges for a firm's core businesses. Corporate venturing would not be the establishment's innovation panacea, as many had hoped.

Spinnovation

Ironically, even as managers were urged to innovate internally far more aggressively, they were being advised by others that intrapreneurship was too limited an approach. Innovating *outside* the bounds of their existing organizations was an even quicker, more flexible, and richer innovation option. If there was a seeming contradiction in the concurrent popularity of these two ideas (internal venturing versus spinouts), it was lost in the excitement of the times. Spinouts became almost as hot a topic as corporate venturing.

As the Internet spawned proliferating dot-com startups in the late 1990s, for example, corporate executives were urgently advised that they could only hope to compete by taking radical action. They were advised to, literally, compete "outside the box," the "box" being their existing corporate structure. Established companies could spin out Internet versions of themselves and beat startups at their own game. The thinking was that the core established firms simply couldn't (or shouldn't) try to internalize the radically disruptive Internet. The old and new technologies, cultures, and business models were just too dissimilar. The entire hierarchy of the parent firm just didn't get it (whatever "it" was) and, therefore, was far too stodgy and slow to adapt.

Spin it out, however, and it was an entirely different ball game. This required setting up a new and separate organization, giving it a life and a label by attaching ".com" to the corporate moniker, and then (most importantly) spinning it out and setting it free. Only if it was loosed from the hierarchy and bureaucracy of its corporate parent, even as it leveraged the parent's brand and reputation, could a corporate dot-com be nimble enough to compete in the New Economy. The added bonus was that a spinout could tap into rich sources of new capital outside the corporate parent (including, perhaps, through a blockbuster IPO) to better fund expensive new ventures with less risk and yet greater upside.

With a spinout, the theory went, you could retain the advantages of corporate parenting even while giving the offspring increased freedom, focus, and funding of a truly independent entrepreneurial organization. Watch the spinout's value soar as its entrepreneurial energies are unleashed, and then capture your share of the value created through clever organizational, legal, and financial structuring. The list of corporate dot-com spinouts grew quickly as every old-line retailer pondered its future in the Internet age: Wal-Mart, Kmart, Toys R Us, Staples, and so on. Spinout excitement was not limited to cyberspace, either. In a variety of sectors, spinouts caught on quickly as a promising fast-track solution to innovation funding, organization, and commercialization.

Within a few years, however, the majority of technology boom spinouts clearly could not stand on their own terms. Many of them struggled to find their own workable business models and failed to gain traction in the marketplace. Most were spun back in or shut

down, leaving a trail of less-than-stellar returns and legal and organizational messes in their wake. The problem was not just that they
were dot-coms in a world where the Internet bubble had burst for
everyone. Many of the non-Internet spinouts also met with disappointing fates. Again, exciting new innovation theory seemed to
fizzle in practice.

The real explanation was more complex, of course. Spinouts can
liberate and accelerate tremendous value creation from innovation.
But they need to be done right, and for the right reasons. Spinouts
are not the appropriate commercialization solution for every new
patent, product, process, or channel. Choosing whether and when
to spin out innovation, and mapping and executing exactly how,
both require critical thinking.

Virtual Reality: Patenting, IP, and "Asset-Lite"

The *asset-lite* approach to innovation offered a pitch different from
that of either corporate venturing or spinnovation. The pitch went
something like this: Don't do it (innovation commercialization) either
inside or outside. Don't do it at all. Go virtual. Let someone else do
the heavy lifting. In the New Economy, intellectual property (IP) is
where the real value resides. Build your company around IP assets,
set up smart and aggressive legal and financial structures (e.g., patent
and licensing deals), and the checks roll in. The lure of the IP
licensing, asset-lite model was its contention that you don't have to
actually *do* much of anything tangible—just *own* and *control* the
key intellectual assets and related intangibles. Create a virtual company that rakes in the cash from licensing while minimizing real
cash investment in rusty property, plant, and equipment in order to
maximize return on assets.

Even if you were on the other side of the licensing equation (i.e., the licensee), the IP licensing model still seemed to make sense. You could reap the benefits of others' discoveries by minimizing your own R&D at risk and simply in-license their IP as needed instead. The virtual, asset-lite, IP licensing model seemed like a win-win for both sides.

The reality is that almost no companies were able to radically transform themselves or otherwise build a core foundation around an IP licensing model. Few firms have been able to build a sustainable and scalable innovation strategy centered around IP alone. Most pure IP-based companies, even those that do it profitably, remain small niche players. If raw IP alone were such a mother lode, after all, U.S. research universities would be swimming in royalties. They're not. Even in the heart of the hi-tech economy, the technology licensing receipts of the most elite tech universities constitute less than 1–2 percent of their total revenues.

The pure IP, asset-lite model has considerable limitations. By itself, raw IP has limited value. Knowledge might be power, but it doesn't deliver profits. The bulk of revenues and profits in any industry come from "doing," not just "knowing." Customers pay richly for solutions, not abstractions. Moreover, over the long term, it's difficult to separate knowing from doing. Without actually getting intimately involved in the details of commercialization and competition, it's difficult for an IP-only company to stay in the game—to innovate the next generation of technology and ideas. The bottom line is that improved exploitation of IP offers significant but typically marginal benefits at best, however rich they might seem in the abstract. On the other side of the equation—i.e., as an IP licensee—depending mostly on in-licensing of key innovations from others can leave a company vulnerable to major, unforeseen costs, constraints, and uncertainties.

Both in-licensing and out-licensing therefore require careful strategic and financial consideration. An aggressive and structured IP plan is a necessary *complement* to, but not a *substitute* for, a more comprehensive innovation strategy. In the vast majority of cases, an asset-lite IP-based innovation strategy alone simply won't do the heavy lifting that's required to create and capture most of the potential profits of innovation.

Shared Creation

Some companies thought it would be best to simply share the costs and risks of innovation. The appeal of innovation collaboration led to a proliferation of R&D and commercialization alliances. The logic of innovation alliances was intuitively attractive: Two heads are better than one, and even more heads are better yet. Share the risks and investments while bringing together different sets of complementary knowledge, resources, and capabilities. In turn, reduce overall development expenses, speed time to market, and help more favorably influence and dominate the industry environment. Create a win-win for all the partners involved.

The advantages of innovation alliances often are illusory, however. Their record is weak in many areas. Remember Iridium? Iridium was the global, Motorola-led alliance designed to revolutionize global mobile telecommunications. The technology and investment consortium included high-profile partners and investors from every sphere of high-tech and from countries all around the world. But Iridium filed for bankruptcy in a spectacular, multibillion-dollar flameout in 1999, just a few months after launching service. Meanwhile, more nimble and focused competitors leapfrogged Iridium with simpler and cheaper solutions. The combined innovative power of many, even formidable organizations, is sometimes less than the power of one.

Even successful innovation alliances might not necessarily translate into profits. Most people would agree that Linux, for example, has been a successful software consortium. The catch is that Linux's great success as an innovation alliance is precisely a function of its relatively free and open nature. This, of course, is exactly the conundrum for those hoping to richly profit from it. Open alliances can be great for generating and commercializing innovation, but are not necessarily very profitable for many of the players involved.

Without a doubt, innovation alliances are often essential. But they carry with them many inherent tensions and challenges. Instead of speeding development, they are often slow and cumbersome. Instead of reducing the costs and risks of innovation, alliances can often increase costs, risks, and complexities. Innovation alliances sound ideal in concept. In reality, they inevitably introduce new issues that beg to be shrewdly planned for and smartly executed for the partnership to flourish rather than fail.

If You Can't Build It, Buy It

In the deal-driven climate of the late 1990s, a different and novel approach toward innovation gained great currency. Don't ally, buy! The basic idea: If you can't build it, buy it. Frothy financial markets fueled more technology deals than ever in terms of both total number and total value. Why waste all that time, money, and effort to do the dirty work of R&D yourself? Let others shed the blood, sweat, and tears, spend the cash, take the risks, and make the mistakes. Then, pick and choose and simply acquire one of the winners.

Cisco Systems was the model to emulate. As others tried to imitate Cisco, rushed and inflated bids for hot technology companies soon turned into record-setting, mind-numbing write-offs totaling hundreds of billions of dollars. JDS Uniphase alone wrote off more than $50 billion (as one observer noted, equivalent to the entire GDP of New Zealand). After acquirers spent huge sums, the technologies or markets frequently turned out to be much less feasible or attractive than advertised. Other companies found themselves holding expensive, hollow shells of companies as the targeted intellectual capital of the acquired firm simply walked out the door right after the deal closed. Entire acquisitions were liquidated for a single-percentage fraction of their purchase price or, in some cases, just completely shuttered.

Innovation by acquisition can pay off, but it's a bet that comes with a price. This price includes both the actual premium for the acquisition and all the difficulties and uncertainties of trying to successfully evaluate and integrate the target—its people, culture, technologies, customers, and more. Technology and markets can change rapidly, which can quickly outdate an expensive, big-move acquisition. Furthermore, there's no guarantee that the exact piece of R&D you need will be developed by another firm at all, that it will be on the market at the right time and at the right price, or that it won't already be snatched up by someone quicker and richer. Undue reliance on innovation by acquisition is a very risky bet.

Mixed Results: What Exactly *Is* It?

The saga of Andiamo Systems illustrates well the organizational twists and financial contortions that companies were willing to endure to the end of innovation. Silicon Valley–based Andiamo was founded in January 2001. The company developed intelligent data switches that enabled many disparate storage systems to communicate and unify as one. Most people had probably never even heard of Andiamo before Cisco Systems acquired it for $750 million in February 2004. This was not a typical Cisco acquisition.

It's complicated. The Andiamo transaction represented the culmination of a significant venture investment and ongoing alliance between Cisco Systems and Andiamo. Cisco already owned 44 percent of Andiamo at the time of the acquisition. Moreover, Cisco had been Andiamo's sole venture funder; Cisco initially had loaned the start-up $42 million and subsequently agreed to provide additional funding of $142 million.

For these funds, Cisco had bought the rights to acquire the portion of Andiamo that it did not already own, at some future date. The purchase price might be as much as $2.5 billion in stock, depending on the success of Andiamo's technology and revenues. The acquisition agreement was also cleverly structured to vary along with Cisco's own market capitalization and revenue so as to minimize any potential impact on Cisco's financials.

Beyond the technology and cash, Cisco otherwise had strong connections with Andiamo. In an unusual arrangement, Andiamo and most of its 300-plus employees (many on leave from Cisco) worked in Cisco buildings on Cisco's main San Jose campus. Under various agreements with Andiamo, Cisco was the exclusive manufacturer and distributor of all Andiamo products. Cisco had even been expensing its cash investments in Andiamo as ongoing R&D costs since its original infusion in 2001.

It was a strong and close partnership. Many of the complexities of the relationship were revealed only after accounting rule changes in 2002 required Cisco to more fully disclose its various linkages with Andiamo. It was such a close partnership, in fact, that new SEC rules required Cisco to account for Andiamo as if it had consolidated the company since its initial investment in 2001.

A bit of background is useful to understand these novel arrangements. Prior to the founding of Andiamo in 2001, much of the startup's top management, including CEO Buck Gee, had been Cisco executives. In fact, founding Andiamo was largely their idea, even while still working for Cisco. They also eventually ended up the primary holders of the 56 percent of Andiamo's equity that Cisco did not own. In fact, other than Cisco, Andiamo employees were the only other equity holders. In turn, many of them returned to roles as Cisco executives after the acquisition deal closed. By the time the acquisition was finalized, Cisco hinted that Andiamo's core market and revenues had both been disappointing. Nonetheless, in cashing out their equity stakes, many Andiamo employees effectively received a rich signing bonus for returning to their "former" employer. Of course, "returned" is also a curious term in this case; after all, they never left Cisco's main campus.

Cisco's Andiamo exercise is a fitting example of how far companies were willing to go in pursuit of innovation. Andiamo combined a bit of corporate venturing and corporate venture capital with the concept of the spinout—in spirit, anyway, even if it never actually left the premises. Cisco and Andiamo tied it all together with an ongoing, on-site R&D and manufacturing alliance. Finally, they finished it all with a spin-in acquisition. Companies were willing to try extraordinary things in order to foster and procure new ideas and new technologies.

The Allure of Innovations in Innovation

The question remains: Why did so many good managers chase after what, at least in retrospect, seem to have been so many questionable ideas? Why did so many great companies pursue with abandon each of the latest and greatest innovation fads and fashions? Whatever their flaws in practice, there were at least three key reasons why all these "innovations in innovation" gained so much interest and momentum.

First, and most simply, innovation really had become more important than ever. It wasn't just a slogan or empty words. Heightened global competition meant that established industry leaders were pressured to generate new low-cost ways to compete or ever-more differentiated products and services to preserve their margins. Product lifecycles had accelerated, meaning "new and improved" had to come more often. Paradigm-shifting scientific breakthroughs in computing, communications, and life sciences, among other areas, started to transform the fundamental processes and products of invention in key industries. Radical new technologies threatened to upset existing business models and alter fundamental industry economics. The pressure for greater and faster innovation became a more central fact of business life. Each innovation fad and fashion, in turn, flourished as companies anxiously sought new and improved means to this end.

The second reason each idea proved so appealing is simply because the old model for innovation sputtered; it was no longer working. Everyone knew it. Everyone felt it. It was on the front page of the paper every day. The classic, brand-name, established success stories of yesteryear—truly original and enormously successful innovators in their own right and time—seriously stumbled. R&D labs that had been the envy of their global peers simply no longer produced. From IBM to GM, from AT&T to P&G, the products and services of former technology and market leaders appeared to grow ever-more stale and tired. It seemed like almost every blue-chip company was either reeling from slumping sales or was threatened by some new upstart. Established companies wanted to escape their musty legacies. They needed renewal. Corporations sought a new model for innovation, especially an alternative to their traditional and bureaucratic R&D approach.

The third reason all these innovation fads and fashions proved so alluring is because each really did offer some novel and valuable contribution. Unfortunately, the limitations and qualifications of each approach usually garnered a footnote at best. Executives and entrepreneurs consequently rushed to adopt each new tool or tactic with few inhibitions. Little thought was given to the critical details of application (when, why) or execution (exactly how). Despite these difficulties in application and execution, each concept did offer some fresh and useful new thinking. They were all useful additions to the innovation toolbox. As with any tools, however, their effectiveness depends on the judgment and skill with which they are used.

Mixing and Matching Tools and Tactics

Our intent, therefore, is not to debunk or discard any of these approaches to innovation. Indeed, our goal is to help rescue the good ideas from being needlessly discarded. Just as there are value stocks, there are value ideas. Value stocks get their value precisely because they are out of favor, yet they retain substantial, enduring intrinsic worth. Likewise, we believe all these innovation tools and tactics, despite having lost their initial luster, offer real, lasting, and essential advances in thinking about innovation.

However, none is the singular solution so often hoped for. No one approach can ever be a one-size-fits-all or cure-all solution for the variety of innovation problems confronting different firms in very different circumstances. Even a single given firm typically is a diverse portfolio of ventures, in different industries and at different stages of their respective lifecycles. Yet, what most often has been prescribed are universal templates extrapolated from a single anecdote or idiosyncratic exemplar company. Managing innovation frequently became driven by the pursuit of some superlative best practice, without considering the context and limitations of the particular approach. If everything could be reduced to a simple formula, innovation would be unremarkable and routine. It's clearly not.

Our practical approach is that context and contingencies matter. Antibiotics are great for fighting bacteria, but they won't do anything to kill the common cold virus. A glass or two of wine per day might improve your health and extend your life span, but binge drinking most certainly has the opposite effect. Innovation fads and fashions tended to ignore such judgment, selectivity, and balance.

What's more, each of these innovation prescriptions had a core problem. They tended to address superficial symptoms instead of underlying causes. The patient was left temporarily feeling better even as his fundamental health deteriorated. Future chapters discuss this critical core problem in greater depth and detail. It is a central issue for diagnosing what went wrong with the application and execution of each new idea, and for building and implementing a better model for innovation.

Innovation is a strategic and organizational problem as much as a technical or creative one. This is another key lesson of the past few years, and a central message of this book: The *how* matters as much as the *what*. Even Enron and Webvan had some good ideas. But their timing and execution certainly lacked. The message is that *how* a company chooses to pursue innovation has profound implications for its success. The choice of strategy and organization (e.g., venturing or spinout, alliance or acquisition, etc.), and its execution, determine whether a good idea flourishes or fails as much as the inherent worth of the idea itself. The *how* determines whether questionable ventures get terminated in good time and good order, or are instead allowed to swell to become enormous boondoggles. Quite simply, success or failure depends on exactly how a company chooses to pursue innovation as much as on the basic idea or invention itself.

Venturing, licensing, alliances, acquisitions, and spinouts therefore all have critical roles in the innovation mix. Knowing when and how each has its place in the mix and when and how to implement each is the critical knowledge. Learning from the ups and downs of each innovation idea requires more critical thinking about when and how these models apply and—just as importantly—when and how they do not. Applied for the right purposes, at the right time, and in the right ways, all of these tools and tactics can help build a more comprehensive innovation strategy and robust overall innovation portfolio. Rather than chasing the latest "magic bullet" or panacea, managers must understand all the different tools available in their innovation arsenal, when and how to use them, and how to combine all of them for maximum effect. The end game is to be able to assemble and juggle a more dynamically optimal mix of all these innovation options to create and capture value on an ongoing basis.

Much like assembling a good investment portfolio, superior performance does not come from any single innovation approach. Instead, the enduring worth—a successful, sustainable, value-creating company—comes from assembling and managing the complex and evolving mix of tools and tactics necessary to bring innovation to fruition. This is a critical feature of new and emerging models for innovation, a subject to which we return in the final chapter.

Background and Overview

A considerable amount of background research informs the examples, conclusions, and recommendations in each chapter. Cumulatively, we examined in detail the record of more than 100 corporate venturing and corporate venture capital programs, more than 100 innovation-driven acquisitions and alliances, and more than 50 licensing deals and spinouts each. We explored a diverse range of examples, of organizations of different sizes and from varied industries, during the 5-year period from the end of 1998 through the end of 2003. Innovation enthusiasm began to bubble by the beginning of this time frame. In many different media, new innovation models were being proposed and then implemented; innovation exemplars were featured and then imitated. Myriad experiments were launched. The choice of a 5-year window was necessary to examine these cases with sufficient richness: to examine their internal and external dynamics and their initial performance, their evolution and ultimate outcomes. A longitudinal examination was necessary to get a better sense of what worked, what did not, and why—i.e., what deeper lessons might be learned.

Except where otherwise cited, our data primarily comes from first-hand sources: conversations and interviews with company founders, executives and former executives, investors and partners, internal company memos and documents, press releases, formal filings, and so on. During the research process, we also reviewed the available innovation literature to better highlight and explore prevailing theories and examples. Where secondary sources are used for more in-depth support or detail, they are cited accordingly.

Here's the typical pattern: A new "innovation in innovation" was announced with great fanfare and introduced with great hopes and expectations. Exemplar companies were recommended as models and used as templates. Sooner rather than later, however, the results of these innovation experiments tended to be far less than satisfactory, and much less exemplary. Even when many of these innovations did succeed in a narrow, short-term sense, they often did surprisingly little for their parent companies from a broader, long-term perspective. The innovation initiatives then tended to be quietly "back-burnered," shut down, or sold off. Retrenchment followed and the cycle soon began again. Meanwhile, the parent organization's core innovation typically suffered and overall performance deteriorated. It's a fundamental and important question: Why do so many supposed "best practices" in innovation so often disappoint? Why does innovation "best practice" so often not work out well in practice?

Some of the individual cases we discuss could fill an entire book. In fact, a few of the examples have been the focus of one or more books. Although such in-depth case studies have obvious benefits, their limitations are also notable. Readers might be left wondering: Is this particular case, however rich and in-depth, the exception or the rule? How and why (or not) does any of this apply to my company and my industry? Were the outcomes simply the result of good (or bad) luck, or is there something more here? In fact, much of the problem with innovation fads and fashions was exactly that—idiosyncratic, exceptional cases were used to extrapolate rules and recommendations for a wide variety of firms, big and small, in myriad industries and situations. They were not designed to engender critical thinking.

This intentionally is not our approach. In covering so much territory, it is impossible to thoroughly delve into each example. In each chapter, therefore, we try to focus on the most important details, the critical variables and their effects, and major conclusions and recommendations. Our intent is to engage in critical analysis that helps lay a better foundation for managers' own strategic thinking and bottom-line approaches toward innovation. For the sake of brevity and clarity, each chapter especially focuses on analyzing in greater detail some of the most celebrated exemplars of each innovation idea. More critically revisiting these examples invariably generates interesting and useful postscripts and more complex but constructive lessons to learn. In most cases, the exemplars themselves were already struggling with their own novel approaches toward innovation, even as many other companies were only just beginning to be advised to mimic them.

Each chapter ends with a summary of key lessons learned based on our broad overview of each innovation in innovation. In the concluding chapter, we tie together all these lessons to help advance a new model for innovation—one that is more nuanced and complex, but also better-grounded and more durable.

2

CORPORATE VENTURING
Best of Both Worlds or Venturing Too Far?

"If you put a circle around Silicon Valley, it would look a lot like Enron. But it's easier to innovate at Enron, because we have a lot less friction."

—*Jeffrey Skilling*

Silicon Valley's success during the 1990s helped further stimulate an already surging interest in corporate venturing. The basic goal of the corporate venturing movement was to emulate and simulate a venture capital–driven startup model within much larger, more mature and established companies. Silicon Valley was the prototype. The challenge was to bring this sort of entrepreneurial energy inside the corporation—even to better it. Pursuing a "simulated startup" approach required significant changes in the old ways of doing business, so much so that it necessitated the establishment of separate, quasi-autonomous venturing structures and divisions within the parent company.

These new venturing units, including independent R&D "skunkworks" and new business incubators, distinguished themselves from the old-line bureaucracy and hierarchy in several key respects.[1] Beyond being separate organizations within the parent company, they inherently required

- New and different methods of leadership, management, and organization.

- New and different techniques to attract and retain talent, to foster creativity, and fuel ideas.

- New and different approaches to budgeting and funding, including risk management.

These factors were key not only to realizing corporate venturing's promise. They would also prove to be primary sources of its many difficulties in practice.

For companies struggling with everything from disruptive new technologies to stagnant sales and declining industries, corporate venturing seemed an attractive prescription. By the end of the 1990s, companies rushed to set up new venture units almost literally overnight. Brash, up-and-coming managers and quirky technical and creative talent were quickly assembled, along with a copious mix of cash and cubicles and computers. The startup units were often physically located off-site in their own gleaming new facilities, in digs more fit for their bold New Economy mission. Some companies went a step beyond and decided to locate their corporate venturing efforts in far-off places, such as Palo Alto or San Francisco or wherever else was hot and "techno" at the moment. In industries ranging from construction to telecom to consumer goods, in companies as diverse as Bechtel, British Telecom, and Procter and Gamble, corporate venturing took on an urgency.

Corporate venturing was presented as an imperative, not a choice—as key to corporate salvation, not a minor or peripheral R&D initiative.[2] The startup model seemed to work so well at powering innovation, after all, especially for technology-fueled, knowledge-intensive, industry-transforming new ventures. It was the genesis of so many business legends and represented the essence of the entrepreneurial success of Silicon Valley and all its imitators. Why not bring these ingredients inside a larger, more mature company to instill a similar sort of creative, fertile, incubating, "intrapreneurial" environment? Why should only young upstart firms generate all the excitement and energy, attract all the world-class top talent, and hatch all the hot new ideas?

The startups' gains were especially galling because established firms had such tremendous leverage in the form of ongoing R&D, cash, brands, customers, and other significant resources. Established companies needed to be able to unleash this tremendous leverage to beat the aggressive, but still fragile, startups who sought to challenge them. The message of corporate venturing was that being a "dinosaur" or an "elephant" wasn't necessarily bad at all, as long as you could be a nimble and adaptive beast, a lean and hungry behemoth. The goal was simply to have the best of both worlds: startup and corporate, entrepreneurial and established, young and old. This was something that even the best of startups-from-scratch could not match.

Breaking the Old Molds

Internal corporate venturing initiatives typically had several key goals. To achieve these ends, corporate venturing units distanced themselves from the established organizational structure. They were separate and distinct from the parent company's hierarchy and bureaucracy, its history and culture, its processes and standard operating procedures. The theory was that creation of such fresh intrapreneurial environments would enable the birth and growth of innovations that never would have been born or that would have simply died on the vine in the old establishment. Establishment of these new organizational subunits would remove hierarchical and political impediments to the advancement of frame-breaking new ideas; they would eliminate the anti-innovation biases of bureaucracy: "You can't do that!" or "We don't do things that way around here." They would attract, nurture, and retain imaginative talent from both within and outside of the company. The new freedom would empower the best employees to accelerate the generation of new inventions and commercialization of new businesses.

Beyond just management and organization, corporate venturing pioneered new approaches toward funding, budgeting, and risk management for corporate development. The nature and needs of startups differed from those of traditional business development functions. The message was: Reconsider, revamp, or even eliminate established budgets and procedures. Provide internal risk capital, VC-like funding. Just as importantly, establish the same type of equity and high-powered motivational rewards and incentives that employees could expect in a real startup; for example, give them "phantom" stock and options to simulate a startup's equity-fueled culture. Traditional, measly year-end bonuses simply would not do the trick.

With the new organization in place, set your top-notch executives, scientists, engineers, and creative talent loose. Let them plant a bunch of real innovation options and watch as they grow. Then, much like the Darwinian processes of the traditional VC/startup model, use periodic reviews, milestones, and funding decisions to prune the underperformers and nourish the promising ventures further as the future unfolds.

Unfortunately, the Darwinian process applied to corporate venturing programs themselves. The featured advantages of corporate venturing—autonomy, risk taking, outside-the-box thinking—turned into liabilities. Once again, Enron was the corporate venturing leader, only this time on the downside. After a string of disappointing outcomes, and in some cases outright financial and strategic disasters, a whole host of companies in a wide range of industries curbed their commitment to corporate venturing or shut down their venturing units entirely. Where did the theory go wrong?

Don't Just Act Like One: Be a Venture Capitalist

A complementary vision of corporate venturing went considerably beyond the notion of establishing new venture units, R&D skunkworks, or internal business incubators. The more encompassing notion of corporate venturing was the idea that established corporations also could—and should—*literally* become venture capitalists. They should establish venture-capital funds to invest chunks of corporate cash into promising new ventures, whether inside or (more usually) outside the firm.

During the 1990s, with companies increasingly envying the rich financial and strategic success of VCs, the idea of corporate venture capital (CVC) exploded.[3] According to the National Venture Capital Association, the number of CVC deals jumped from just 126 in 1995 to more than 2,150 in 2000, while the total dollar amounts surged from $400 million to $17 billion. For its part, of course, Enron had four of its own venture-capital funds.

Targeted corporate venture capital investments promised not only great direct financial returns, as with traditional VC investments. They also offered the potential of even greater-leveraged synergies with the parent, both strategic and financial. Through CVC, corporations could more quickly discover new technologies and new businesses. As they developed and grew, CVC investments would allow corporate investors to have an inside track on partnering with or acquiring these startups' innovations. Companies as diverse as

AT&T, Eastman Chemical, GE, Intel, and Time Warner became widely touted corporate venture capitalists.

As CVC funds grew in popularity and resources, they made bigger and bigger investments and ventured further into more diverse types of businesses. Their growth in size and breadth was an attempt to tap into even more novel ideas, further diversify their strategically targeted portfolios, and reap greater financial gains. "Complementary" became the criterion or catchword to sum up these more broadly targeted CVC-funding activities. The definition of complementary grew broad in practice, with computer firms investing in health care startups and consumer goods firms investing in e-commerce companies. These types of investments were made with the logic of spurring new applications and new markets that might in turn enhance the funding firm's own products and services. The objective was to create a more fertile industry macroenvironment or ecosystem in which the parent company could flourish.

The Ups and Downs of Corporate Venturing

The efforts of Andersen Consulting (now Accenture) provide a quick glimpse into the peak of CVC enthusiasm. In December 1999, the global information technology and consulting powerhouse launched Andersen Consulting Ventures (ACV), a new CVC unit focused on investing in business-to-business electronic commerce companies. Andersen committed more than $500 million from its own funds and sought to raise the total to more than $1 billion by soliciting investment from other outside VC funds and financial institutions. The founding of ACV even merited a brand-new Palo Alto office—quite a stretch from Andersen's Midwestern, buttoned-down global headquarters in Chicago.

Andersen planned to be more than a passive investor in ACV. Instead, the company would be a strategic investor and active partner, using its IT, consulting, and management expertise to help power

ACV's portfolio companies to success. In an interesting twist also being adopted by other corporate venturers, Andersen even allowed payment for services rendered in the form of equity. ACV soon joined forces with other new CVC funds that were also focused on electronic commerce, including Commerce One Inc.'s Commerce One Ventures, founded in August 2000.

Andersen's timing could have been better, but it was hardly unusual. Its late start, near the top of the venture capital boom, is typical of CVC in general. Just 2 years after its founding, along with a slew of other now-withering CVC efforts, Accenture announced it would sell Andersen Consulting Ventures. The announced reasons for the sale: to reduce volatility in earnings, and to allow the company to refocus on its core businesses of IT and management consulting. Accenture took a $212 million charge for losses on ACV investments, causing its second quarter 2002 profits to drop 87 percent.

In September 2002, Accenture reached final agreement for CIBC World Markets to buy its venture portfolio. Accenture would retain just 5 percent. At the same time, Accenture reaffirmed "it would discontinue direct venture capital investing and no longer accept illiquid securities from clients or alliance partners." Accenture would leave VC investing to VCs.

Accenture's story was a microcosm of larger, longer-term CVC habits and trends. According to the National Venture Capital Association, CVC investments peaked at nearly $17 billion in 2000 and plummeted to less than $1 billion in 2003. The number of deals peaked at nearly 2,200 and dropped to just over 300 during the same time period. In 2001, Microsoft recorded more than $5 billion in losses from its venture investments. Intel lost more than $600 million. AT&T, Compaq, News Corporation, and many others abruptly decided to simply shut down their CVC efforts.

What goes up can come down. With the high potential upsides of CVC come the real possibility (if not likelihood) of low downward swings. It was easy to forget this as financial markets and startup valuations kept soaring ever-higher. Ironically, the much touted logic that corporate VCs were supposed to be more "strategic" and, therefore, more patient about their investing—that is, compared to those flighty, quick-buck financiers—proved false. Corporate VCs were first to the exit door. Again, venturing theory seemed to go awry in real-world practice.

The Disappointing Record of Corporate Ventures

Corporate venturing has a spotty long-term record, one only punctuated by the excesses of recent years. Each of the individual elements of corporate venturing and CVC by itself seems to make sense. They appeared to work beautifully in the Silicon Valley model. Combined in a corporate context, however, these elements most often did not produce, or caused unintended and unfortunate results. Many companies sharply curtailed or shut down their ventures, skunkworks, and incubators and shut down, froze, or sold off most or all of their CVC portfolios.

History would suggest that these results were likely, if not foregone conclusions. Corporate venturing more often than not had produced weak results even prior to the recent technology boom and bust. Few people recalled Exxon Enterprises's unfortunate corporate-venturing experiences in the 1970s and 1980s, for example. Just as it would seem years later to many other companies, the logic seemed sound at the time: to help Exxon better exploit the voluminous output of its massive corporate R&D efforts and to help it generate and invest in new products and new markets, from both inside and outside. The losses piled up into the billions before Exxon jumped ship. After experimenting with everything from solar and nuclear power to information systems and office equipment, Exxon's venturing ambitions ran out of gas and were completely junked.

Some of the more hopeful recent examples fared little better. Throughout the 1990s, from the major airlines' repeatedly failed ventures into discount "airline-within-an-airline" concepts (e.g., Continental Lite and United Shuttle) to General Motors's Saturn experiment, corporate venturing had a lackluster record. Each initiative was launched with great fanfare and considerable investment. Soon, each was sputtering, quietly swept away, or simply abandoned.

In general, the record for corporate venturing and corporate venture capital actually was relatively much better before the corporate-venturing concept really took off as a fad in the later 1990s. The collapse of the bubble only accentuated the hurdles that venturing efforts faced, especially when hurriedly and uncritically implemented. As the authors of *The Venture Imperative* admitted, "Most companies have tried some form of corporate venturing, and most companies have failed at it."

The implication of most critiques and analyses of corporate-venturing missteps was to the effect of "if only companies could do it better . . . ." But the difficulties of corporate venturing go much deeper than implementation. They are inherent in the concept itself. They are part of a larger "core" problem.

Reconsidering Corporate Venturing Success

Despite their featured successes, even some of the most widely touted recent exemplars of corporate venturing had their notable troubles. During the height of innovation excitement, the three most frequently and prominently featured examples of corporate venturing were Enron, Xerox, and Lucent Technologies. By 2000, literally hundreds of books, articles, and case studies cited their corporate-venturing prowess as models from which to learn.

There definitely were lessons to be learned from these examples, though not always the ones intended. The disastrous results of the Enron experiment speak for themselves: collapse, bankruptcy, lawsuits, and all the rest. The corporate venturing performance of Lucent and Xerox are different stories, but are still sobering in their own ways. In their Five Year Shareholder Scorecard, for example, *The Wall Street Journal* cited Lucent and Xerox among its "Worst Performers" from the end of 1998 through 2003. Lucent, in fact, was number one on the "Worst Performers" list with an annualized compound average total return of –41.6 percent. Xerox did slightly better at only –24.3 percent per annum. Of course, much of this record was because of the massive technology and market downturn, but the other 998 companies on the *Journal*'s scoreboard also went through the same wrenching period. What had happened to all Xerox's and Lucent's fabled corporate venturing successes? Why weren't they reflected in their stock prices?

These post-hoc results highlight a critical point that must be kept in mind for other would-be corporate venturers, and for assessing the overall record of corporate venturing. It is not enough to look at the short-term success or failure of individual ventures alone, although the record is also weak in this regard. Corporate venturing ultimately must be assessed by measuring its impact on the corporate founder and funder (i.e., the corporate parent). More accurately assessing corporate-venturing performance, much like assessing the performance of venture capitalists themselves, requires gazing over a broader and longer-term horizon, not just pointing to a single small venture. In this regard, it's useful to review the record of Xerox and Lucent to see what lessons a more holistic retrospective might offer.

Complex Lessons from Venturing Exemplars

The justifiably acclaimed Xerox Palo Alto Research Center (PARC) has long been one of the most well-known and precocious pioneers of innovation as an R&D "skunkworks" or innovation "hothouse." As Xerox badly sputtered in the later 1990s, however, not many would-be corporate venturers gave much attention to the mixed lessons that Xerox's PARC experience offered. Instead, even more ambitious R&D skunkworks and new venture incubators were launched and pushed full speed ahead. The now widely known tale is that, despite Xerox's lavishing resources on PARC over the course of three decades beginning in the early 1970s, many of PARC's most famous inventions never turned into successful and profitable innovations for the parent company. Xerox's PARC was a tale of massive missed opportunities (*Fumbling the Future*, one book was titled).

Without question, PARC was very successful as an R&D skunkworks; it was a prolific font of all sorts of hardware and software inventions and path-breaking new ideas in the areas of computing, communications, graphics, and the like. PARC developed various early versions of the personal computer (PC), user-friendly graphical computer operating systems, the Ethernet, and numerous laser-printing technologies, among a long list of other credits. Its contributions to laser printing were the most notable single success story for parent company Xerox. Although Xerox did not directly gain from many other novel inventions and technologies, some of these other PARC innovations were brought to market through a succession of spinout companies. Xerox Technology Ventures (XTV), one of the pioneering and most active dedicated corporate venture capital funds, facilitated the process of bringing PARC technologies further toward commercialization.

In the final analysis, however, the fantastic genius and prolific technology output of PARC could not and did not revive, revamp, or rescue Xerox's deteriorating core businesses. Xerox was not able to take PARC's ideas and inventions and use them to reinvigorate itself, even though it was at least theoretically possible that they might have done so. Now, it's probably not fair to fault PARC or Xerox Technology Ventures for not reviving the entire company. But some of the more vigorous promoters of corporate venturing would have us believe precisely that—that such novel "innoventuring" is a key, if not the key, solution to the core problems of corporate innovation. If such outstanding efforts and incredible wellsprings of innovation like Xerox PARC and XTV cannot do the trick, what possibly could?

By the end of the decade and in the wake of serious competitive and financial difficulties, Xerox began to seek outside investors and customers for PARC to try to make it a self-sustaining, independent company. Subsequently, Xerox laid off much of the staff and considered whether to entirely spin off PARC. If Xerox and PARC were such exemplars of corporate venturing, why was the parent company severely downsizing the research center and even questioning its future as part of Xerox? Despite its myriad inventions and patents, PARC offered Xerox little hope.

Inherent Venturing Problems

Most diagnoses of PARC's problems fault Xerox executives for their lack of vision and bumbled management. But it's possible there's something more fundamental at the root of its problems. Much of the problem was in the nature of PARC itself. PARC's autonomy and freedom were critical factors in fostering the creative and dynamic environment that generated so many new ideas. Yet this libertine independence was also a key factor that made it so difficult for PARC to be a catalyst to revive or transform Xerox's core businesses. Many of PARC's concepts were fabulous advances in their own rights, but were a bit off-the-mark—in reality, perception, or both—for Xerox's core needs. Some of the common problems of "Not Invented Here" repeatedly surfaced. PARC researchers in Palo Alto clashed with Xerox R&D personnel and product development executives in New York and elsewhere around the world. PARC and Xerox's other core global R&D and product development efforts were, both literally and figuratively, quite far apart. PARC was very creative in the abstract, but not nearly as *effective* in practical business terms.

One lesson from even this relatively prolific experiment in corporate venturing is the limitations of pouring massive amounts of talent and resources into quasi-autonomous R&D skunkworks or new venture incubators. Such investments, even if thriving in their own right, might nonetheless do little to resolve a company's larger, more important innovation challenges. Brainstorming, creative genius, and being on the cutting edge often mean being "out there," literally and figuratively, on the periphery. Internal venturing R&D skunkworks or venture incubators might generate myriad new ideas and inventions. Regardless, their net contributions to a company might be marginal. They might be largely irrelevant or relatively insignificant in terms of the core strategy and direction of the parent company. Even good and useful venture-generated ideas might be difficult to integrate with the parent: strategically, organizationally, technologically, culturally, or otherwise.

Lucent's New Ventures

The venturing experiences of Lucent Technologies also offer some valuable insight in this regard. During its relatively brief existence, Lucent's New Ventures Group (NVG) garnered much attention as a model for corporate venturing. It had some notable successes in terms of individual ventures. From a broader perspective, the record is more interesting and nuanced.

Lucent's famed Bell Labs R&D operations had always generated more inventions and ideas than the parent company knew what to do with by itself. As Lucent split from AT&T in 1996, some of Lucent's new management saw this excess innovation as an opportunity, not a problem. They imagined that, even if they were not always a clear fit with Lucent's main lines of business, Bell Labs's many patents and inventions could realize tremendous value if they could somehow be pushed further toward commercialization. Bell Labs had long since run a significant licensing operation to externalize its technology. Bringing more ventures to fruition more fully and quickly required a different approach, however, if Lucent were to be able to create and capture greater value.

After some initial experimentation with a few ventures during 1996 and 1997, the Lucent New Ventures Group was officially formed in late 1997 and early 1998. In addition to Lucent's own initial contributions, by 2000, the NVG attracted $160 million in outside venture capital funding for its various technology ventures. By 2001, the NVG portfolio included more than two dozen companies, the vast majority of which were direct offspring of Bell Labs research.

Despite NVG's successes, Lucent itself sputtered and tumbled as the telecommunications industry crashed. By the end of 2001, Lucent's NVG was being prepared for sale. New outside investments from Lucent's own corporate venture capital arm (Lucent Venture Partners) also dried up. Even as the company's approach to corporate venturing continued to be featured as a model, was the telecom crash prematurely forcing Lucent to give up on a good part of its future (its notable venturing experiments with NVG)?

Lucent's own assessment had become more mixed. In the midst of an ongoing strategic and financial crisis, exacerbated by the continued weakness of the entire telecom sector, Lucent felt it could no longer afford such wide-ranging and distracting experiments. The company embarked on a massive retrenching, restructuring, and refocusing.

Lucent's Ex-Venturing

In January 2002, Coller Capital bought the NVG, with Lucent retaining just 20 percent. Likewise, investments by Lucent's CVC arm ended abruptly: "In early 2002, Lucent Technologies made the strategic decision to limit the activities of Lucent Venture Partners, in an effort to focus its resources on the internal developments that best serve its large service provider customers. As such, Lucent Venture Partners will no longer pursue new investments." Lucent's top management decided that it lacked the logic and resources to keep supporting the NVG as well as active venture capital investing.

Juggling dozens of new ventures requires significant time, attention, due diligence, and patience. It requires careful funding and ongoing nurturing. As was the case with both Lucent's NVG and its Lucent Venture Partners, and also the case with Xerox PARC and Xerox Technology Ventures, the mission of such organizations typically is to support innovations that are not central concerns of the parent company. Investments focused on innovations that fall outside the parent company's own core technologies and markets. Despite the successes of Lucent's NVG in launching new startups, it did little to alleviate the core strategic, competitive, and financial challenges of the parent company. This is not that surprising, given that it was not really designed to do this in the first place.

However, this very fact raises some fundamental questions: What is the purpose of such corporate-venturing efforts if they are not "core" to the company's success in the first place? If this type of venturing is not something that the parent feels compelled to continue pursuing to ensure its future, what is the underlying logic for it to begin with? A simple financial justification seems inadequate. There are many other potential ways to realize value other than through such non-core, full-scale internal venturing experiments.

A good example of the complex issues involved comes from Coller Capital's purchase of Lucent's NVG itself. The acquisition highlights questions about the purpose and competence of operating companies being involved in non-core venturing and venture capital activities. Coller Capital, a London-based private equity firm and venture funder, formed New Venture Partners (NVP) to manage the former Lucent NVG portfolio it had purchased. Almost all NVP's management team consisted of former Lucent-affiliated managers. Just a month after NVG was sold, a new transaction sparked some surprise and controversy. In February 2002, Coller Capital earned back more than the price it paid for the entire Lucent NVG by selling just one of its portfolio companies, Celiant, for $470 million.

Did Coller get the best of Lucent? Was Lucent unaware of or unable or unwilling to pursue the true value of its own portfolio of ventures? Whatever the case, Coller's clear and aggressive focus on running a financially successful venture fund quickly seemed a more lucrative approach than Lucent's.

Other Ex-Venturers

A year later, in a similar replay of Lucent's experience, Coller Capital purchased four companies of BT Group's (formerly British Telecom) three-year old Brightstar technology incubator. Coller established a new fund, NVP Brightstar, in which BT retained a minority 23 percent interest. NVP Brightstar also gained exclusive rights to create new startup businesses using BT's intellectual property portfolio.

British Telecom's Brightstar initiative was originally designed for much the same purpose as Lucent's NVG—to help commercialize the copious output of BT's R&D labs. Nine companies were founded or spun out, and more than $50 million in external VC funds were raised. By the time of their sale, however, none of the ventures had earned any payback for BT through a liquidity event such as an IPO or acquisition. Continuing this venture "outsourcing" trend, in October 2003, Coller's New Venture Partners (NVP) announced a similar deal with Philips Electronics. NVP was tasked with identifying and facilitating possible venture spinouts from Philips's R&D labs and intellectual property portfolio.

None of these results suggest that corporate venturing efforts, such as Xerox PARC and Lucent's NVG, and their corresponding corporate venture capital funds (Xerox Technology Ventures and Lucent New Ventures) did not have clearly identifiable successes in their own right, on their own terms. They birthed some important technology and several successful spinouts and, in that sense, generated positive economic value. In reviewing Xerox's and Lucent's widely acclaimed corporate venturing efforts in terms of their broader and longer-term performance, however, one must also consider the larger context. From this perspective, corporate venturing failed to deliver, even for some of its most celebrated practitioners.

Corporate venturing was, the theory went, the primary or sole hope for large and mature companies to stay strategically, competitively, and financially fit. Corporate venturing experience seems to offer a more mixed and cautionary message. Don't go looking for company salvation—or even substantial rejuvenation—in corporate venturing. You're likely to be disappointed. The odds were stacked against corporate venturing because of the very strategies, structures, and processes by which it typically was pursued.

The Consummate Corporate Venture Capitalist

A final example helps illustrate both the possibilities and uncertainties of the corporate venturing model in general, and corporate venture capital more specifically. Intel Capital, the venture fund division of Intel, has prospered as one of the largest, best-known, and most successful corporate venture capitalists. No company's CVC efforts garnered as much attention as Intel's.

Intel Capital started small in the early 1990s, making investments primarily in other semiconductor companies or semiconductor design software or equipment makers. The company typically invested as part of a syndicate that included other, more traditional VC firms. The professed goal was to invest in companies and technologies that would help accelerate and expand the performance and possibilities of Intel's own core products.

As the technology boom picked up steam throughout the 1990s, Intel Capital expanded its horizons to invest in a much wider variety of computing and communications ventures, both hardware and software, broadband and wireless, Internet and telecom. The stated goals remained similar if somewhat broader: to enhance the speed and growth of key markets for the parent company and its products. In 1999 alone, Intel invested $1.2 billion in nearly 250 new outside ventures. By the end of the year, its portfolio consisted of about 350 companies. In 2000, the investments paid off handsomely as Intel recorded a one-time gain of $2.1 billion. Even as the technology bust spiraled downward, unlike many of its fair-weather imitators, Intel Capital continued active, if somewhat diminished, venture capital investing.

Intel's position as a CVC role model is ambiguous, however. Its most prominent successes seem more of an exceptional historical case, not necessarily a template that other firms might readily follow. Intel Capital's own boom period, for example, occurred during a unique period characterized by the explosion of the PC, Internet, and related computing technologies. Intel was at the center of each revolution. Its quasi-monopoly microprocessor profits allowed it the luxury of being able to afford to invest excess cash into myriad peripheral, or "complementary," activities in a way the vast majority of other companies could never hope to do. In this sense, it was relatively easy for Intel to establish and support a sustained CVC program, even with the inevitable ups and downs, including a billion in losses in 2001 and 2002. Few other firms, other than extraordinarily rare and valuable specimens such as Microsoft, could really fit such a rich model. Intel's privileged position gave it unique power in its product markets and in financial markets. It had better information and better access, unparalleled clout and influence in order to take advantage of venture investing opportunities like almost no one else could. Its most fantastic gains were in the bubble years of 1999 and 2000, when all technology investors looked pretty smart—at least for a moment.

One key assumption about Intel Capital's purpose and performance, apart from its financial contribution, remains questionable.

On the strategic side, Intel Capital's investments primarily have not been in Intel's own core technology domains. Instead, Intel Capital intentionally invested in what it termed "complementary" new technologies and businesses in order to foster a richer "ecosystem" for its products. Which key markets for Intel's core products would not have blossomed without Intel Capital's investments? This is largely a hypothetical question, of course. But from an economic and technological standpoint, one can build a reasonably strong argument that Intel Capital's boost to these markets was uncertain at best.

On one hand, for example, Intel Capital professed to help build a "Wi-Fi ecosystem" through its venture funding. But, on the other hand, Intel CEO Craig Barrett noted around the same time, ". . . WiFi didn't happen because Microsoft or Intel or Cisco said it was going to happen; it happened because a bunch of grassroots folks just said, 'Hey, this is a cool thing.' The PC emerged the same way."[4] Likewise, the explosion of the PC industry in the 1980s and early 1990s—the single event that fueled Intel's success more than anything else—far predated the existence and investments of Intel Capital.

In contrast to this ambiguity, what is beyond dispute is that Intel's continuing success as an industry-dominating technology company was due to its massive, ongoing core R&D and manufacturing investments and its core new business development initiatives. For example, Intel's Celeron provides a good counterpoint to the arguments for the necessity of corporate venturing as being key to corporate innovation. Of Intel's recent innovations, few were as radical and as important as Intel's decision in the mid 1990s to make and sell lower powered, lower priced Celeron microprocessors. Intel's business model had been built primarily around the reverse approach—ever-higher powered chips and big boosts in prices to match. Yet, Intel's Celeron was not born in some clandestine skunkworks and commercialized in a venture incubator. It was not something discovered, funded, and acquired through Intel Capital, Intel's massive CVC operations. Instead, Celeron was a core innovation initiative seized upon, and frantically pushed forward, by Intel's top management and entire organization—including especially CEO Andy Grove. It was a central R&D and management focus that helped significantly enhance Intel's continued dominance in microprocessors. Other important initiatives, such as the later family of Centrino mobile/wireless chips, also followed this non-venturing model.

The bottom line is that Intel's enormous innovation success was fundamentally not a function of either corporate venturing or corporate venture capital. Intel's investments in core R&D and manufacturing totaled greater than $8 billion in 2003 alone. This was more than eight times the entire amount of CVC invested by all companies in all industries that year. For those interested in finding a new font of bottom line–boosting corporate innovation, Intel Capital was not necessarily much of a guide. Intel Capital's prosperity was more a *byproduct* of the parent company's enormous R&D, strategic, and financial momentum, not a fundamental cause or key source of its success. Correlation is not causality.

Core Problems with Corporate Venturing

So why does corporate venturing so often fall flat? By examining more than 100 corporate venturing efforts, we identified several recurring issues. By itself, each issue can cause considerable difficulties. In combination, as they most often operate, these issues can lead to intractable problems and outright failure. Many of these problems revolve around problems related to *focus* and *fit* or, relatedly, *scale* and *scope.* The end result might be that, paradoxically, even "successful" corporate venturing can be a net value destroyer.

- **Irrelevant?**—The innovation or venture might be exciting and novel, but not particularly relevant to the overall mission, strategy, and core businesses of the parent firm.

Brainstorming is great and is often a primary goal and key output of corporate venturing. But ideas too far removed from the technologies and markets of the parent firm might be largely irrelevant, even if they are potentially valuable to someone else. Firms cannot abruptly jump to operate in businesses in which they have no particular resources, competence, or advantage. The infamous venturing of Exxon Enterprises into office equipment is one of the most glaring examples of this. Many people later cited the same problems with Enron's venturing into broadband. Further-reaching, ever-stretching novelty is often the essence of corporate venturing, but such novelty does not equate to profitable business models or sound strategic directions for the parent.

- **Immaterial?**—The new venture or corporate venturing effort might be successful in its own right, but not particularly material for the parent company. Even several successful ventures might cumulatively have only small impacts on overall corporate performance. Independently incubated startups take time and nurturing to get to scale; sometimes, it takes over a decade to have a material impact for the parent firm. In other cases, corporate venturing creates only small niche businesses. This is what, by its very nature, corporate venturing tends to generate. Much of Lucent and Xerox's venturing efforts often seemed to fall into this category. (We address these critical issues of relative size and growth later in this chapter.)

- **Distraction?**—Corporate venturing can give false hope and unduly divert attention and resources. Venturing can be a fun and exciting diversion. After all, who wants to deal with the old, tough, intransigent problems of the core business? But in the end, it can be a dangerous distraction that draws attention and resources away from a firm's more central tasks and critical challenges. No company can juggle innumerable strategies and opportunities. Not even the richest companies can successfully fund and manage an infinite number of ventures. Companies must make strategic choices. They cannot cast about the seeds of myriad innovation options and then simply see which ones flourish or fail. Each venture requires intensive nourishment and care or else *all* of them will fail. This means that firms must make exclusive, defined, limited strategic choices and then commit to them. Firms that focus too much on newfangled venturing often tend to ignore and neglect their real revenue and profit-generating businesses. The core continues to decay regardless of—or even *because of*—aggressive venturing. GM's Saturn fits this category. The major airlines' discount startup ventures (Continental Lite, United Shuttle, Ted, Song, and so on) also largely appeared to be distractions as unrelenting cost issues and losses continued to trouble their mainstream airline operations.

- **Detraction?**—The distraction issue links directly to the ultimate performance question for the parent company. The bottom line is that even a successful venture effort might detract from the corporate parent's overall performance. Even a venture with positive net present value by itself might actually *destroy* value when it's considered in a larger context. Attention and resources diverted to corporate venturing might leave the firm as a whole in worse shape than before the venture. Failed venture efforts, of course, make the situation even worse by both distraction (such as lost time, talent, market share, and continued troubles in the core businesses) and direct financial losses.

All these factors might combine to result in net value destruction for the parent company. It's not just coincidence that many examples of corporate venturing feature initiatives that are interesting or novel in their own right, but are hardly large and powerful engines of corporate growth to boost core revenues and profits. In contrast, even a minor distraction (e.g., resulting in just a 1% drop in Intel or IBM's share price) might result in billions in lost value. That's a lot of ground to make up with even a big bunch of successful little ventures.

Limitations of Venture Scale and Growth

The limitations of even successful but still relatively small ventures highlight a related core problem with corporate venturing, especially for large companies. Huge differences exist between a Fortune 500 company and a new startup. Much of it is a problem of relative *scale* or *size* and relative *growth*. What looks like good initial marketplace success and fantastic growth for a new startup might be either immaterial or quite disappointing for a much larger, more established company. A young startup getting to $10 million in sales is a fantastic achievement in entrepreneurial terms. Doubling sales to $20 million and reaching profitability is even more impressive. For a $1 billion company, however, a $10 million increase in sales is much less exciting. What looks like a promising beginning and great potential from a startup's point of view might disappoint a large, established company by being too little, too late.

From the parent company's point of view, the tangible and intangible costs in terms of diseconomies of scope (scattered or squandered time, attention, resources, and so on) might exceed the relatively small benefits of incubating and funding many small, disparate new ventures. They might become more of an annoying and draining distraction rather than a promising portfolio. Lucent and Xerox decided the benefits were not worth the costs of maintaining such extended, disparate venture portfolios.

At a minimum, incubating to sufficient scale even greatly promising new ventures takes patience and forbearance. Hip discounter Target is one of the most successful retail ventures in recent years, for example. Old-line department store chain Dayton Hudson completely transformed itself over time to the point where its Target division accounted for more than 75 percent of sales and profits. In 2000, the company even formally changed its name to Target Corporation in recognition of this transformation. Of course, Dayton Hudson had opened its first Target store in 1962. This transformation was hardly an overnight venturing success story.

Growing new corporate ventures to scale won't always take that long, of course, especially in an era of accelerated growth and change. To grow something from scratch, however, will almost always take significant time and considerable investment, often more on both counts than many firms are willing or able to commit. The only way to greatly shorten this time and lessen the required investment is to pursue innovations directly aligned, or readily able to be integrated, with an established firm's existing core business—its core R&D and technologies, products and processes, customers and markets, brands and features. Scaling up quickly under these circumstances is a more tractable task of integration, not the more risky and laborious burden of full, stand-alone incubation from scratch.

Venturing's Alignment and Integration Problem

Unfortunately, corporate venturing does not excel at aligning and integrating innovation with the core of an existing firm. Corporate venturing inherently tends to be placed outside the mainstream and distinguishes itself as apart from the parent organization in so many ways. This situation highlights some of the intrinsic strategic, structural, and organizational difficulties of corporate venturing.

Take Wingspan Bank, for example. Bank One founded Wingspan as a stand-alone Internet bank venture. The initiative garnered much attention. With this bold experiment, Bank One seemed to leap ahead of its banking peers in transitioning to the New Economy. After a quick and seemingly promising takeoff, however, Wingspan quickly lost altitude. Enormous advertising and technology expenditures failed to make it soar. Moreover, Wingspan directly conflicted and competed with Bank One's own mainstream online and off-line banking efforts. Wingspan folded by mid 2001 and its accounts were simply absorbed into Bank One. The net result of the experiment? Many observers noted that Bank One seemed to have significantly fallen behind its peers in online banking.

Even in the radical technological upheaval brought about by the Internet, newfangled corporate venturing was not the approach of the vast majority of successful corporate innovators. Most corporate players who made successful, sustained, and profitable transitions to the Internet Age did not set up some separate Internet incubator or new web venture divisions. Instead, companies such as Dell and Southwest Airlines integrated radical innovation and made the Internet core to their respective business models and corporate strategies.

Can You Be Too Free?

Corporate ventures' strategic, structural, and organizational problems often stem from their inherent autonomy. Autonomy was one of the key levers of corporate venturing efforts. It was their primary reason for being. By definition, corporate venturing requires establishment of separate, quasi-autonomous structures and organizations. The goal is to give new ventures the leeway to be unboundedly creative and entrepreneurial. Autonomy is also the problem, however. The end results of such freedom can be unintended and undesirable. In this regard, corporate-venturing activities also frequently suffer from one or more of the following syndromes:

- **Neglect?**—Corporate ventures that are outside of the mainstream and, therefore, off the headquarters' radar might easily become neglected. After much initial fanfare, many corporate venture efforts soon fade from view and are starved of attention and investment. The parent firm's top management does not have the time, willingness, or resources to bother with the venture. Ventures might suffer from a "stepchild" syndrome. Key people and assets might suffer from attrition. Even ventures with great potential wither. When the parent encounters tough times, venturing efforts are often the first to suffer the biggest cuts—even if they hold out the most long-term promise. GM's Saturn fell into this category. After massive investment, great fanfare, and notable initial success in the marketplace, the tap ran dry. Crucial years passed before any substantial reinvestment went into pushing out new models. Saturn went from being a rising star to a being a bit of a dog.

- **Conflict?**—Venturing units might end up, intentionally or unintentionally, in direct conflict with R&D and business units from the mainstream of the parent organization. Instead of focusing on outside competitors, both the venture and the established parent unit might focus on attacking each other for scarce resources. Both venture and parent units might battle to sell to the same customers and partner with the same partners. Customers and collaborators get confused. The logic of internal competition sounds good in theory, but often ends up in duplication, higher costs, and lower performance for both the original parent unit and the venture itself. Many new internal Internet venture units faced this dilemma as they catered to the parent's existing customers (for example, Wingspan Bank), with the only real difference being the online channel format.

- **Not Invented Here?**—Even if no *direct* conflict exists between the venture and the parent organization, a Not Invented Here (NIH) syndrome can cause difficulties. NIH might be a technical problem, an emotional problem, or both. Autonomy means that the venturing unit is disconnected from the firm's normal R&D and business development processes. NIH feelings on the part of those in the parent organization simply might indicate that the venture's innovations are widely off-the-mark; they don't meet the company's needs or specs. On the other hand, even technically useful corporate venturing might suffer from a more emotional, two-way NIH bias. Those in the venture view the parent organization as stifling and backward. Venturers typically want to start fresh and new with their inventions and ideas—even to pursue them outside the parent firm altogether—rather than tap into the firm's existing resources and capabilities. Meanwhile, those in the parent organization view the venture folks as a bunch of overpaid, arrogant upstarts—or even worse, as direct threats. (In some of our cases and interviews, managers and engineers specifically cited intentional sabotage of ventures because of such ill-will and related dysfunctions.) Knowledge does not get shared and cross-fertilization is stifled between the venture and parent. Even good ideas might be ignored or trashed instead of transferred and nurtured.

Politics and personalities take over. Venturing efforts ranging from Xerox PARC to GM's Saturn found themselves in this situation. Enormous potential learning either was technically off-the-mark or even good ideas were squandered because of "softer" but contentious internal dynamics.

- **Out of control?**—The autonomy of corporate venturing might cause financial, organizational, and sometimes even legal difficulties. "Corporate budgeting kills innovation," the warning went. Normal budgeting, control, and risk-management procedures might be suspended or altered to give corporate ventures more freedom to experiment with radical new things, accelerate their funding and development, and attract and retain top talent. If everything works well, that's great. But Murphy's Law often takes over and venture freedom turns to chaos. Unfortunately, the parent usually remains liable for the chaos that its ventures create. Enron, of course, is the exemplar in this category. Many of its corporate ventures should not have advanced beyond the brainstorming or experimental stage. But supposedly old-fashioned management controls were ignored. In fact, these controls were scorned and ridiculed and replaced with supposedly "cutting-edge" budgeting, valuation, and risk management techniques more fit for the New Economy. High-upside rewards and incentives for venture managers (e.g., deal-based bonuses, phantom options, etc.) can worsen this situation by perversely promoting extreme risk taking. Of course, Enron is an extreme case, but it's far from the only case. During the past few years, many investment boondoggles have involved such (literally) out-of-control venturing.

Diverging Approaches Toward Cars of the Future

GM's Saturn division typifies a combination of these problems: distraction, detraction, neglect, and NIH. As a brand-new attempt at transformational innovation, Saturn initially had great success. With billions in new investment—a new physical location, new plant, and so on—General Motors established Saturn as a novel and completely separate division. The primary intent was to help GM make and sell small cars that could better compete in quality and features with Japanese imports. A secondary objective was to experiment with an entire host of new ideas to try to help GM learn and rethink the way it made and sold cars. In the early 1990s, Saturn quickly gained many fans, including customers and industry analysts. Its reengineered manufacturing techniques (e.g., more "enlightened" and participative labor practices) and novel use of materials (e.g., plastic, no-dent body panels) and its fresh, more customer-friendly marketing and sales (e.g., flat, "no-haggle" pricing) all gained accolades.

Before Saturn could even move on to a new base model or brand extension, GM became distracted and neglected Saturn. Lingering problems within the company's core and an upturn in lucrative pickup and sport utility vehicle sales diverted GM's attention from Saturn. Saturn languished, with few new products and a waning critical and customer fan base. Sales began a long, hard slide. Management and labor turmoil ensued. Corporate learning was limited. Perhaps not surprisingly, GM's overall small-car and sedan offerings also continued to flounder. Many of Saturn's much-touted innovations—from materials to marketing—were never adopted by other divisions of the parent company. Instead, R&D and design, materials and manufacturing, management and labor, and sales and marketing approaches from GM's other operations began to seep into Saturn and started to transform it into just another (troubled) division of GM.

The development and launch of Toyota's and Honda's hybrid (gas-electric) cars provides a contrasting example. Electric power was supposed to be a profoundly disruptive technology for the automobile industry—a classic and compelling sign of the need for corporate venturing. Yet, Toyota and Honda responded in a different fashion. Their gas-electric hybrid ideas and related technologies were not born and developed in some newfangled, off-line corporate venture. Instead, these initiatives represented core R&D and executive commitments to new power sources, fuel efficiency, and environmental responsibility. In particular, Honda's efforts were not at all "outside the box." In fact, its first mass-production gas-electric hybrid took the unremarkable form of a classic Honda Civic. Toyota's Prius likewise helped it gain a lead of at least a couple years in commercializing this fairly radical (if not in appearance, in locomotion) alternative to the traditional automobile.

An Established Operating Company Is Not a VC Portfolio

Beyond corporate venturing broadly defined, corporate venture capital itself raises other specific issues about the nature and purpose of corporate venturing. One key difficulty with uncritically applying a VC/startup-like approach to the needs of corporate innovation stems from the fundamental differences between an established operating company and an equity investment fund that invests in startups. Quite simply, an operating company is not a venture capital firm. Some analogies just don't fit.

The primary goals, resources, and capabilities of a successful, established operating company are different from those of a successful, independent, financially driven venture-capital fund. Fundamentally, operating companies are not purposed or designed to fund and nurture many diverse and far-flung startups, especially those whose technologies and businesses are not of demonstrable material concern to the parent firm's core business. A VC's guiding logic is inherently financial. In contrast, an operating company's guiding logic must be strategic, even if a key end is to ultimately produce good financial results.

There's a reason why VC funds typically have long life spans, for example. Normally, initial VC investments take quite a while to pay off. In the short term, cash mostly flows out and even write-downs and write-offs occur as some early venture investments inevitably stumble. This negative volatility is standard for VC firms; the big gains come years later. In contrast, larger publicly held operating companies operate on continuous budgeting and reporting cycles (such as quarterly revenue and earnings estimates and reports). Severe volatility is frowned upon and rudely punished by financial markets. For operating companies, a tension always exists between short-term operating planning and performance and long-term investing. This tension can test the patience of even the most farsighted corporate managers. When the going gets tough, many CVCs get cold feet and quickly exit the venture capital business almost as quickly as they rushed into it at its peak.

Risky, long-term bets on uncertain new technologies or businesses, especially those that fall outside the parent company's focus, are difficult for many companies to justify and sustain. In theory, more "strategically oriented" corporate VCs can and should be more patient than supposedly fickle, purely financial VC investors. The empirical evidence shows otherwise. In practice, because of the realities and constraints of running a real company, corporate VC investors tend to be much less patient. This only exacerbates their losses, as they perversely tend to bail during the worst times.

"Strategic" Corporate Venture Capital

The consistent message of the empirical evidence and accumulated experience is that corporate venture capital efforts are more likely to be successful when they do not stray too far from core *strategic* goals aligned with the purpose and focus of the firm's core businesses.[5] CVC efforts need some freedom and autonomy to roam and explore cutting-edge investments. Simultaneously, they must be kept anchored. Being strategically guided does not imply that such investments do not need to make sound financial sense as well. Even the greatest strategic ideas can be senseless at the wrong price. In this regard, Intel Capital's mission statement has the right balance: "Make and manage financially attractive investments in support of Intel's strategic objectives."

It's easy to make such a mission statement. Virtually any company could adopt almost a word-for-word motto for their own CVC program. It's the judgment and execution of this balance that causes difficulties. In practice, what exactly are the strategic and financial bounds? What is, or is not, really a strategic investment? Enron Broadband Ventures invested in a wide variety of seemingly unrelated web startups, from entertainment providers to online talent agencies, all with the strategic logic that they would help provide content for Enron Broadband. Beyond strategy, exactly what are the financial criteria and objectives by which to manage a corporate VC fund? Should they be more liberal or more constrained because of the parent firm's directive to pursue strategic investing?

A strategic logic for corporate VCs introduces other challenges that professional, independent VCs simply do not confront. Independent VCs diversify their portfolios in multiple ways; they do not have the directive to support any specific company's strategy. This reduces their risk and increases the returns of their portfolios. Most VCs can make emotionless, sectorless decisions about what to buy, what to keep, what to sell, and what to kill. For strategic CVC investors, this logic does not apply. The strategic directive is a good guide in its own way, but from another perspective, it's also a ball-and-chain. Strategic investing implies that the fund's investments are focused and constrained, and therefore are relatively undiversified. For CVCs, this implies a forced choice between either taking on more systematic risk (correlated not only within their own portfolio, but also with the parent firm's core businesses) or ignoring the strategic logic to diversify into more distant and unknown territory.

Strategic CVC investing also sets up potential conflicts with funded companies in ways that independent venture capital does not. Unlike independent VCs, strategic CVC funders want something from their investments beyond just lucrative financial returns. They want early and privileged access to new ideas and new technologies that help the parent company. They want an early scoop and favorable terms on being able to license, partner with, or acquire if a funded startup should hit it big in one way or another. These parental interests raise strategic, organizational, and financial dilemmas that independent VCs simply do not have to deal with. Inherent conflicts exist between the interests of strategic CVC funders and the distinct interests of startups in maximizing their own success. A startup may want to pursue more and different partners, for example, or want to shop itself around and sell to the highest bidder.

To address such conflict-of-interest concerns, many corporations establish internal "walls" that completely separate the parent company and its CVC fund. Such walls prevent the parent from having privileged access to, or undue advantage over, the funded startups. The dilemma of these arrangements is that they remove the compelling strategic logic for companies to fund CVC investing in the first place. If companies gain no special privilege or advantage or information by investing, what's the point of investing?

None of these tensions and challenges alone is reason to abandon the concept of corporate venture capital. However, all of them must be addressed for success. They must be carefully balanced in order for CVC activities to function well.

More Mature CVC Approaches

Not surprisingly, the more successful corporate venture capital programs both predate and survive the most recent CVC boom and bust. The pharmaceutical industry provides several good examples of these more balanced, eclectic, and patient approaches. For example, GlaxoSmithKline's S.R.One was founded as a wholly owned, venture capital affiliate of SmithKline in 1985. S.R.One has separate offices and management, including a non-disclosure policy (except otherwise with permission) between S.R.One and GSK regarding any of its portfolio startups. By 2004, S.R.One cumulatively had invested nearly $400 million in over 100 companies (such as Amgen, IDEC, Sepracor) and continued to actively invest. Beyond achieving good financial returns, S.R.One's guiding mission was to invest in companies of potential collaborative interest to its parent. This meant investments in health care, primarily in pharmaceuticals and biotechnology. In addition, GSK also invests in other more diverse (but still health care–focused) ventures through participation in outside-led, independently managed venture funds, such as Euclid SR. Johnson & Johnson, Eli Lilly, Merck, and other pharmaceutical majors have pursued similar carefully balanced and eclectic CVC strategies. Firms in a variety of other industries also have managed to do so with reasonable success, including companies such as Eastman Chemical and its Eastman Ventures unit.

Aligning Funding with Focus

Even within such relatively successful efforts, most CVCs have increasingly recognized their own limitations. As corporate venturing and corporate venture capital interests expand beyond the core domains of their parent firms, greater "outsourcing" is both useful and appropriate. This means soliciting greater involvement and investment from professional, independent VC firms and other types of outside partners. Even if originally developed in the parent company's own R&D labs, for example, non-core innovations are often best funded and managed with someone else as the lead—not the parent. Both the parent company and the partner(s) might reap considerable benefits, while allowing each party to focus on what it does best. The agreements between Coller Capital and Lucent, BT, and Philips are good examples of such an approach.

For core innovation needs, companies that focus too much enthusiasm on corporate venture capital might be led to ignore the myriad other ways available to tap into the energy and ideas of the startup world. An established company need not invest a single cent of corporate venture capital in order to do so. Many of these alternatives are more focused and direct, and yet more flexible; they might help a company avoid some of the key drawbacks of CVC investing. As we discuss in the next few chapters, companies can pursue direct investments in startups; co-development agreements with startups that provide initial seed funding and then periodic milestone or progress payments; targeted joint ventures or structured licensing agreements; and a whole host of other options. These alternatives tend to be more directly guided by and linked to the core R&D and business-development needs of the parent company, and therefore tend to be more successful.

Smart companies always have directly or indirectly invested in innovative young upstarts with great strategic and financial promise; this concept is nothing new. The growth of the more formal concept of corporate venture capital is what is relatively new. Yet, the old approach of direct investment sometimes can be more effective. With direct corporate investment in young innovators, for example, there is less of the strategic-versus-financial conflict of using more formal corporate venture capital funds. Instead, either the corporate treasury or individual divisions themselves can make direct investments and manage them much more clearly for the growth and success of the investing firm's relevant core businesses.

Do You Have to Pay to Play?

In many other ways, without investing a single dollar in direct venture capital funds, a company still can proactively and strategically tap into the vast and dynamic innovation networks represented by the larger VC community and its myriad funded startups. In fact, there's little reason why most companies should not be aggressively engaged in these networks in one fashion or another. Even with zero direct CVC investment of its own, a company still can tap the vibrant energy and ideas of VC-fueled innovation.

By actively monitoring and communicating with VC-led innovation communities, smart companies can continually scan and sense important developments in their respective technology and industry environments. They can actively be on the lookout for new ideas and intelligence, new technologies and products. They can seek early and favorable access to potential innovation licensors, alliance partners, and even potential targets for future direct corporate investment or outright acquisition.

How do such strategies work? These cash-poor but idea-rich CVC strategies recognize the recurring reality that venture capital often is better handled by independent, professional venture capitalists, not directly by operating companies. Yet, they simultaneously recognize the reality that there is enormous value to be discovered in VC-fed innovation networks.

Take IBM's recently evolved (and still evolving) approach to corporate venture capital. IBM does have substantial investments in numerous outside, independently managed VC funds. But these investments are relatively passive and indirect. Based on its own recent experience and learning, IBM struggled to find a compelling strategic logic for pouring massive amounts of capital into its own, directly managed CVC funds. Instead, IBM decided to tap into VC-fueled innovation using a more indirect, but still very active and strategic, approach. Using a series of VC "relationship managers" in different sectors, IBM continually and proactively communicates to the wider VC community its critical current, and projected future, technology and innovation needs. IBM's strategy helps energize a network of dozens of friendly and interested VC firms who then, on an ongoing basis, help IBM locate and tap into the relevant VC-funded innovations and innovators as they come to fruition.

Why and how does this type of creative but cash-poor approach to corporate venture capital work? It's a simple win-win scenario. IBM gets its technology and innovation needs and wants communicated widely and aggressively, and therefore better and more quickly fulfilled. In turn, VCs and their funded startups get favorable access to an incredibly rich customer, strategic partner, or potential acquirer—i.e., IBM. Without investing a single cent in direct venture capital, a company need not (and should not) forgo the rich potential benefits of tapping into vast and dynamic VC-driven innovation networks. IBM tries to keep a core focus on what matters—fueling its core businesses with new and necessary innovation. It does not focus on directly dabbling in disparate VC investments, however exciting and novel that may seem. Ironically, IBM sometimes even finds itself the potential (preferred) partner or acquirer for startups funded in part by its competitors' CVC funds.

In effect, what happened in 2001–2003 was a return to more normal, rational, level-headed views of corporate venture capital. Interest in CVC continued to be high, but corporate approaches to this latest "innovation in innovation" were now more cautious. In 2003, for example, the total number of CVC deals and number of companies invested in remained almost double the level of the mid 1990s. However, according to the National Venture Capital Association, CVC dollars represented only 6 percent of total VC funding, down from a high of 16 percent in 2000. Moreover, total CVC investments were equivalent to just one-half of 1 percent of overall corporate R&D spending. These investments continued to play an important role in the whole innovation mix. But CVC's surprisingly small proportion of the total amount invested reflected a belated acknowledgment of the limited function of corporate venture capital in solving the core problems of corporate innovation.

The Need for *Core* Venturing

The overall message is not that corporate venturing is a futile cause. Instead, the message is that corporate venturing as it is so often practiced is not a panacea for the innovation challenges of large and established companies. We only suggest the usefulness of a more sober view of its limitations and its possibilities, its downsides and its upsides. Being more aware of, and proactively planning for, the common problems of corporate venturing helps increase the chances of success of venturing efforts (see Table 2-1).

Table 2-1 The Promises and Problems of Corporate Venturing

	The Promise/The Theory	The Problem/The Reality
The Logic of Corporate Venturing		
Autonomy	Start fresh and new—almost like a real startup! Freedom to be unboundedly inventive and creative. Escape the stifling, musty old bureaucracy and hierarchy. Dynamic internal competition.	Inventions and ideas that do not fit the strategic focus and priorities of the parent company. Irrelevant or immaterial ventures. Internal conflicts, dysfunction. NIH syndrome. Distraction, detraction, neglect of core.
Rewards and incentives	High-powered incentives—almost like a real startup! Attract and retain the best talent. Motivation and enthusiasm. For example, "phantom" equity, options, "mark-to-market" bonuses.	Resentment, dysfunction, attrition from personnel in the mainstream organization. Extreme (undue) risk taking. Short-term focus, deal-making, "cash out" mentality.
Funding, budgeting, and risk	"Corporate budgeting kills innovation." Need to foster risk-taking. Use novel, looser funding, budgeting, risk-management mechanisms to let ventures experiment and flourish—almost like a real startup!	Normal, prudent decision making and risk management are ignored as being irrelevant or inappropriate. Misalignment of risk and reward: An established company has much existing value at risk, unlike a startup. Lack of controls, out of control. Increased risk, loss of value, followed by reaction and (undue) risk aversion.

(continued)

Table 2-1 The Promises and Problems of Corporate Venturing (*continued*)

	The Promise/The Theory	The Problem/The Reality
The Logic of Corporate Venture Capital		
Strategic investing	Invest only in areas where the parent firm has special needs, knowledge, and capabilities. Realize enhanced synergies between parent and startups to create more value. Increase the odds of success for both startups and parent.	"Strategic" can be used to justify almost anything, whatever's hot at the moment. Less-diversified "strategic" investing increases firm's overall financial risk. Strategic investing raises dilemmas and conflicts of interest between corporate funders and funded startups, potentially hampering both parties.
Financial rationale	Share in high, VC-like returns of 25 percent or more per annum. Diversification of innovation options and profit streams. Formal CVC funds are the best way to manage corporate venture investing. You've got to "pay to play" the VC game.	Most VC funds do worse than market indexes; a small minority make the big bucks. "Buy high, sell low": CVCs tend to enter at the peak, pay high prices, and then exit quickly in a downturn and sell low. High (firm-correlated) volatility: High upsides are matched by low downsides. Direct (non-CVC) investing sometimes is a more focused and better aligned strategy. You don't necessarily have to "pay to play": Tap into VC-fed innovation networks with "no money down."

The bottom line is that, rather than a company stagnating and losing its edge because of a *lack* of corporate venturing, it's possible for a company to lose its way and destroy value precisely *because* of its corporate venturing. Corporate venturing in practice has frequently been a misplaced focus. Paradoxically, it's typically inherent in the nature and structure of corporate venturing to neglect or impede core innovation, not advance it. Value creation through innovation needs to be at the center of the organization, not at the periphery; core innovation must be the focus. Ultimately, this determines overall firm performance and decides a company's success or failure. Corporate venturing efforts therefore need to be closely aligned with and readily integrated into a core innovation strategy. We return to this issue a little later.

3

THE VIRTUAL ASSET-LITE MODEL
Intellectual Property Licensing

"To the winner of the race will go possible Nobel prizes and huge potential profits."

—*The Genome Gold Rush*

"Priceline will reinvent the DNA of global business."

—*Jay Walker*

The advent of the New Economy created another twist on innovation. It wasn't just a New Economy; it was now a Knowledge Economy, too. The concepts of innovation and intellectual property (IP) became inextricably intertwined. The most valuable venturing was virtual—building a firm around IP. Patents were the strongest form of currency, not just onerous paperwork. IP licensing was no longer

67

viewed as a mundane legal process. Instead, it was a core corporate strategy and a legitimate, lucrative business model. It was *the* key to realizing the potential riches of innovation.

The new IP licensing model for innovation was predicated on the basic beliefs that knowledge is power and IP equals profit. Organizing for innovation therefore meant going virtual in a very real sense. Focus on creating and capturing key intangible assets. Protect and license and leverage them. Minimize real investment. Maximize real profit.

It seemed almost anything was patentable: raw ideas, business processes and business models, even life itself. New companies gained huge valuations on the basis of their novel patent portfolios, not necessarily because of their sharp and innovative operating businesses. In Priceline's case, one key asset was U.S. Patent No. 5,794,207—bilateral buyer-driven commerce—better known as *name your own price*. The IP excitement was much broader than just the Internet. Innumerable genomics companies sprouted to patent the unraveling mysteries of human DNA, for example.

A patent machine became the preferred prototype for a Knowledge Age startup. At the same time, old-line companies, such as IBM and Xerox, were cited as transitioning to new, IP-centered strategies, reaping rich gains and transforming themselves in the process. For 1991, IBM had an already impressive 679 patents granted. A decade later, that annual tally had soared five-fold to 3,411. Both types of companies, new and old, served as models for the New Knowledge Economy.[1]

The Old Economy: Real Companies, Real Products

Until the past decade or so, licensing played a relatively minor role in most firms' innovation strategies. It was largely an afterthought. Licensing one's own inventions to others (out-licensing) had been a reliably, if marginally, lucrative operation for some firms for many years. On the entrepreneurial front, occasionally, there was some Horatio Alger story of the lone, idiosyncratic, garage-lab inventor who struck it rich after winning a legal battle against big business and signing lucrative licensing rights for some newfangled contraption. For the most part, however, patenting and licensing remained a routine and unglamorous activity. Licensing was often viewed as more trouble and expense than it would be worth or was relegated as a tactic for old technologies in secondary markets.

Patents themselves were not viewed as something to be aggressively and proactively commercialized. They were not the essence of innovation, nor were they the key to realizing its value. Instead, patents were a formality and technicality. They were used primarily as a defensive legal tactic to protect and defend one's inventions, and to keep other firms from getting hold of and unjustly exploiting one's own R&D without paying their due. Patenting was a game of denial—to deny competitors traction, to threaten and frighten them, or to pull the rug out from under them if infringement had already taken place. It was a reactive process driven and executed mostly by attorneys. IP management was not a game that most executives and entrepreneurs dreamed of or particularly wanted to play. The real business of innovation continued to revolve around actually transforming the abstract ideas embodied in patents into cold, hard reality: creating, manufacturing, and selling real new products. IP licensing was not a core part of the innovation commercialization strategies of established and successful firms.

On the other side of the equation, few successful companies would have even considered licensing the inventions of others (in-licensing) as an integral part of their core innovation strategies. In-licensing had a stigma attached to it. Although it was perhaps occasionally and regrettably necessary, in-licensing was a second-class approach. It highlighted a firm's own inability to do the real, hard work of R&D. It left a firm at the whims and mercy of others, not in full control of its own destiny in terms of the critical function of invention. In-licensing was like an involuntary tithe that, even worse, might flow directly into the coffers of a more innovative competitor.

Intellectual Property Rules

Times change. The rise of the New Economy brought with it the ascendance of the intangible, in both substance and style. Even with their incredible legacy of innovations and long list of patents to match, the old "smokestack" manufacturing industries had long dominated the economic landscape not so much with their IP as with their extensive real property, plant, equipment, and labor. The paradigm for the emerging knowledge-intensive, technology-driven economy was different.[2]

A new model of innovation, value creation, and company building gained currency. It was no longer about empire building; instead, it was about virtual empire building. Enron CEO Jeffrey Skilling famously exemplified this new attitude as he promoted the new paradigm of the *asset-lite* firm. It was no longer about commanding and controlling physical assets. Creating and capturing value from innovation now centered on the ownership and rent-seeking exploitation of intangible, knowledge-based estates. According to the U.S. Patent and Trademark Office, the number of patents granted annually nearly doubled during the 1990s (99,077 in 1990 compared to 183,975 in 2000), as did the number of patent applications (176,264 compared to 315,015).

It's difficult to imagine now because management fashion changed so much and so fast, but the concept of an IP-centered business model just a short while ago would have been a curiosity at best. Mostly, such an idea would be met with quizzical looks. An observation from that time offers a glimpse into the rapid and profound change in mindset: "Patents on business methods used to be a rarity, because it seemed legally preposterous to claim ownership of a way of doing business."[3] Beginning in the mid 1990s, however, the U.S. Patent and Trademark Office broadened its own notion of what was patentable, a move subsequently backed by the U.S. courts. Managerial and entrepreneurial thinking dramatically changed as well. The virtual land grab began. The idea of an IP-centered model for creating and capturing the value from innovation became not only widely known and accepted, but even a preferred ideal.

Virtual Assets, Real Profits

The knowledge-intensive, asset-lite approach to innovation commercialization offered a sweet-sounding pitch. The pitch went something like this: Go virtual. Let someone else do the heavy lifting. In the New Economy, the real value resides in IP. Build your company around IP assets, set up smart and aggressive legal and financial structures and processes, and the cash will flow. Many enthusiastically touted such asset-lite approaches even for what had been thought of as old-line businesses (e.g., Enron's transforming a stodgy pipeline company into a dynamic energy-trading and derivative operation).

Central to this new paradigm was a shift toward the idea that innovation's profits spring forth not from real, hard, and tangible assets, but instead flow from ownership and control of key intangibles, such as patents and processes, and software and standards. Physical assets increasingly became thought of as commodities, mundane (if necessary) base materials upon which intellectual capital could work its Midas touch. For leading companies anyway, plant and equipment would be largely passé. Manufacturing was the toil of lesser mortals, admittedly necessary but relatively low value-added work. After all, the dirty job of manufacturing could easily be outsourced for the lowest cost.

The big bonus of the IP-centered, asset-lite approach was that it promised to make financial statements sparkle. With intangible IP itself as a company's core product, relatively little direct incremental "cost" exists in terms of a company's cost of goods sold (COGS). That is, after the base IP is developed and paid for, each unit's incremental cost is miniscule, often near zero. Compared to the old way of doing business (invent-build-sell) in which each unit has very real and substantial costs attached to it, IP gross margins look fantastic. Moreover, the leverage of increased sales is enormous; beyond recovering the initial R&D costs, it's mostly thereafter pure profit.

So began the great patent race. Patent anything and everything. For entrepreneurs, patents became the high-tech equivalent of lottery tickets. Buy as many tickets as possible to cover your bets and at least one of the numbers would surely hit big. A few companies did hit it big, at least initially, even if their novel, sweeping patent claims proved more than slightly controversial and contestable.[4] Meanwhile, established companies were accused of negligence for letting their extensive patent portfolios gather dust, leaving supposedly trillions in license royalties unrealized. Corporations rushed to dust off their forgotten and neglected "treasures in the attic" to rediscover, assess, and collect their true value. New and old companies, ranging from biotechnology to software, scrambled to stake their claim on everything from the fundamental structure of the human genome to the basic points-and-clicks of e-commerce.

Ins and Outs of Licensing

Fortunately for the new and enthusiastic out-licensing crowd, in-licensing concurrently and complementarily grew in its appeal. Companies became less and less hesitant to source innovation from outside in a movement toward more "open innovation." Not Invented Here (NIH) lost much of its stigma. In a faster, more complex, and more competitive economy, managers increasingly sought whatever pieces of technology it would take to get the job done, no matter what the source.

An explosion of interest in out-licensing was accordingly matched by a like increase of in-licensing activity. The combination of these complementary out-licensing and in-licensing trends led to a dramatic increase in licensing activity by all types of organizations. Even universities and non-profit organizations jumped on the bandwagon. New IP management divisions and technology transfer offices sprouted. IP-centered consulting and advisory firms proliferated. The number of books and articles extolling IP's unparalleled economic power and enormous profit potential soared. In the net, however, the supposedly radical new IP licensing model for innovation was more evolutionary than revolutionary, and more complex and challenging than its proponents suggested.

IBM = IPM (Intellectual Property Management)

IBM's history both foreshadowed and helped set the key trends in IP licensing that emerged during the 1990s. For most of its nearly century-long history, IBM did not actively mine its unique, enormous, world-class IP portfolio. The company extensively licensed for decades, but this was largely because of antitrust consent decrees that required it to freely provide its many patents and technologies to all who applied. IP licensing revenue was not a principal concern. As IBM's dominance of computing began to erode throughout the 1980s, however, the company started to get more serious about generating revenue from new sources. Its intangible assets and IP portfolio proved an irresistible target.

Even as the 1990s began, IBM was still a net payer for IP. However, its new and aggressive licensing initiative dramatically turned the situation around within just a few short years. IBM licensed not only patents, but complex processes and know-how in fields ranging from computing to communications and software to semiconductors. By the decade's end, IBM's IP initiative generated more than $1 billion annually. Even for an organization as large as IBM, these were clearly fantastic gains on heretofore underutilized intangibles. From 1993 to 2002, IBM booked a total of more than $10 billion in IP licensing revenues.

With these results, it's hardly surprising that IBM became one of the exemplars of the innovation-as-IP-licensing movement. As with so many other innovation exemplars, however, there is considerable ambiguity about whether IBM is the IP example that other firms can or should emulate. Moreover, for those seeking a new model for innovation, IBM does not really offer an entirely new template as much as an evolution toward better IP management. In the final analysis, IBM's IP licensing gains are more a byproduct of the firm's fantastic core innovation success, rather than the source of this success. Consider the following exceptional facts.

IBM might have been at the cutting edge of IP management and technology licensing, but it was hardly a virtual company. It remained a very "real" organization. IBM continued to create and sell real products, services, and solutions—more than $80 billion worth every year. It had more than 300,000 employees and billions invested in hundreds of facilities for R&D, manufacturing, and service worldwide. This is what funded the vast majority of IBM's R&D, which in turn led to an ongoing, virtuous cycle from which excess IP was continuously generated and licensed. IBM's IP licensing represented the "excess" generated by its highly successful core R&D and operating business units, the proceeds of which in turn fed additional incremental resources back into this core.

IBM's licensing revenues are backed by an incredibly deep and broad IP portfolio, the result of massive, ongoing investments in R&D representing a century-old history of innovation. The firm invested more than $5 billion per year in R&D; it cumulatively has invested the equivalent of hundreds of billions. Here's another exceptional statistic: IBM employs more than 5,500 Ph.D.s—just Ph.D.s alone, not total researchers. To get a better idea of the scale of IBM's investment in brainpower, consider that during the 1990s, only about 800 Ph.D.s in computer science were earned annually across the entire U.S.

Even against such a backdrop of massive and sustained R&D expenditures and enormous intellectual and human capital, IBM's IP achievements are still impressive. Each year from 1993 to 2003, IBM received more U.S. patents than any other company in the world, a total of more than 25,000. In 2003 alone, IBM received nearly 3,415 patents from the U.S. Patent and Trademark Office; that's more than any other company in history in a single year. The scale and scope of IP generation was outstanding. Yet, this total still equaled less than one patent per year per Ph.D., and Ph.D.s aren't cheap. Given $5 billion in annual R&D expenditures, IBM's $1 billion of annual IP licensing revenues were hardly easy profits. Given these sorts of facts, IBM's IP licensing achievements are no less admirable. But they certainly appear much more proportional and are much more difficult for other companies to imitate or otherwise use as a simple template. However much its IP programs generate returns, the payoff is not out of scale with the rest of IBM's superlative investments and achievements.

Despite its fantastic success in reaping the rewards of its IP, IBM's awakening did not represent a transition to a radically new and different IP licensing model. Its "real" businesses remained the real revenue and profit generators. In contrast, IBM's IP licensing and related revenues were not a steady growth business by any means. They actually declined by 11.2 percent from 2000–2001 and declined a further 34.2 percent from 2001–2002, even as the company's total sales remained relatively steady.

IBM is certainly not alone in reaping significant gains from more active management of an extensive IP portfolio. Other organizations, such as Lucent and Texas Instruments, have also harvested hundreds of millions or more from their more proactive IP licensing. But, like IBM, these are also hardly virtual enterprises centered only around IP. They are distinguished industry leaders with decades-long histories, tens of billions of cumulative R&D investment, and tens or hundreds of thousands of employees. They have real, multibillion-dollar global investments in everything from labs, manufacturing, and marketing to customer service and support. They make real products and provide real services and solutions. This is the key source of ongoing value creation for even these most exemplary of IP managers and technology licensors. IBM's own technology chief put it well: "[W]e consider patents a starting point on the path to true innovation." IP is the beginning, not the end, of innovation.

The "Knowing" and "Doing" Connection

The bottom line is that so much of the tremendous IP success of organizations like these comes from ongoing investments in actually *doing*—creating, manufacturing, and marketing competitive world-class, market-leading products—not just *knowing*. They do not just think and dream and toil in the labs and then simply license their abstract intellectual output. It is too difficult to separate knowing from doing. Even just recognizing the value of IP, much less actually realizing this value, might require a great degree of practical, applied knowledge, experience, and capabilities. Without actually getting its hands dirty in the nitty-gritty of commercialization and competition, it is difficult for an IP-only company to stay in the game and to innovate the next generation of technology and ideas. A surprisingly huge amount of innovation in many industries originally comes from customers and suppliers, for example.[5] Without being involved in such a value chain, an IP-focused firm cannot learn and gain their ideas, inventions, and insights.

The ideal of transforming a company into a virtual corporation built primarily or solely on raw IP remains elusive in practice except for specialized or niche firms. Even for Microsoft, another often-cited example and the most successful and valuable New Economy company, IP licensing (as opposed to product licensing) remains only a minor operation. One of the key architects of IBM's IP management and technology licensing success during the 1990s, Marshall Phelps, took the same role for Microsoft beginning in 2003. Even as Phelps embarked on revamping and expanding Microsoft's IP licensing efforts, he noted that the company did not expect any direct substantial revenues anytime in the foreseeable future.[6] Instead, Microsoft's newly energized IP licensing initiative was designed to support and bolster the company's other core products and services. It was designed to help create a better support structure, not to be the "main game."

Another IBM transplant, Rick Thoman, tried to replicate IBM's IP licensing success at Xerox. He started as the new Xerox president in 1997 and then continued the task as CEO beginning in 1999. Thoman was hired, in large part, for his IP savvy. He had been IBM's CFO for much of the 1990s, helping encourage and manage IBM's explosion of licensing activity. After taking the helm at Xerox, one of Thoman's key strategic initiatives for Xerox was to replicate, if not better, IBM's success at exploiting its IP portfolio. Xerox already was a rich potential mine, with more than 5,000 of its own patents and processes to license. A revamped IP strategy held promise to quickly help boost Xerox's bottom line. Unfortunately, the initiative did little to help Xerox address its core business problems or halt its continuing slide. After little more than a year as CEO, Thoman left Xerox as the company's problems worsened.

The experiences of Microsoft and Xerox offer a key point to ponder. Even the original architects of IBM's own IP-rich licensing strategy could not readily replicate this lucrative model in other global technology leaders like Microsoft and Xerox. Clearly the odds of doing so were very challenging at best.

The Secret of Life (Patent Pending) Itself

Few areas of the New Knowledge Economy embodied the new IP buzz, the new innovation-as-intellectual-property paradigm, more than the exciting and booming field of genomics. An entirely new industry sector was born and literally dozens of companies were founded on this paradigm that knowledge is power and IP equals profit. In this case, the knowledge was that of life itself, decoding and understanding (and, of course, patenting) the human genome. The human genome was viewed as the Rosetta Stone for unraveling the secrets of health and disease.

The promise appeared to be so great that genomics excitement even survived the technology bubble bursting in March 2000. Genomics firms continued to launch successful IPOs that were still spectacular in their own right. Among other cures, genomics was promised as the salvation for a stagnant Big Pharma. The big drug companies' pipelines dried to a trickle despite their massive increases in R&D investment. The old approach to drug discovery and development seemed to have run its course. A rapid increase in fundamental knowledge of human life itself promised to rapidly bring new power to the drug discovery process. It heralded the advent of innumerable new diagnostics, therapies, and cures. Whoever could own the maps to these treasures and the keys to unlock these secrets would surely harvest untold riches.[7] The new genomics leaders could name their price as Big Pharma scrambled for a place in line to license them.

Human Genome Sciences (HGS) and Celera Genomics were two firms that made the biggest splash. J. Craig Venter, formerly of the National Institutes of Health and the founder of the Institute for Genomics Research, provided the brains for both firms. The pioneer for the industry, Human Genome Sciences, formed in 1992 and went public in 1993 as the first pure stock market play on the mapping of the human genome. HGS was the harbinger of many more similar firms to come. More than a dozen were formed just within a year or so of HGS's founding. Progress was slow, however. The revolution took a while to gain momentum.

The real boom began a few years later. Celera Genomics was co-founded in 1998 by Venter and Perkin-Elmer, the pioneering maker of high-speed, automated DNA analysis equipment. During the later 1990s and into 2000, an entire slew of companies joined the genomics revolution and went public: CuraGen, deCODE Genetics, Exelixis, Genaissance, Genomica, Genset, Hyseq, Incyte, Interleukin Genetics, Lexicon Genetics, Medigene, Millenium, Myriad Genetics, Pharmagene, Variagenics, and so on. Some companies focused their efforts on the raw genomics data itself. The pharmacogenomics players focused on decoding the interaction between genes and drugs. Other firms focused on providing services, software, and support for these decoders. Bioinformatics was born.

Complex Secrets

Genomics quickly proved to be slightly more complicated and evolutionary, and less lucrative and revolutionary, than most companies had planned. By the end of 2002, in a quick turn of fortune, many genomics-focused firms were trading for less than their cash in the bank. Their IP pursuits now seemed like dry wells, not gold mines. Of the big players, Celera Genomics had a market capitalization $100 million less than its net cash. One of the smaller players, Variagenics was trading at a market capitalization of less than half its $50 million net cash. In a move toward consolidation and a bid for survival, some players acquired others not for their IP, but simply for their cash, then shut down or liquidated the acquired firm's operations. Clearly, making money from the Rosetta Stone of the human genome was a tougher business than many had anticipated.

It's important to note that the difficulties the genomics sector encountered were not because of a lack of fantastic scientific advances. Instead, many companies ran into tough times *despite* their amazing new scientific discoveries. Regardless of many accusations of grandstanding and hyperbole, the early genomics discoveries truly did represent fantastically rapid and profound biomedical progress. Some of these advances in understanding were even discussed as being worthy of Nobel Prizes. Celera Genomics claimed to have decoded the human genome, after all. Many of the smaller players discovered specific genes that had significant roles in serious ailments such as cancer, depression, diabetes, and obesity.

A lack of scientific discovery and lack of patents were not the reasons for these firms' troubles. Their troubles also were certainly not because of a lack of active and aggressive IP management, either. They were founded with IP management and licensing as the centerpiece of their strategies and business models. Their difficulties were more fundamental: The problem was simply that the basic science and raw IP had very limited commercial value.

Most of the harbingers of the genomics revolution subsequently radically overhauled their strategies. They chose to focus on developing real diagnostics and, especially, real therapies and cures—not just selling raw data and roadmaps—as where the real profits were to be discovered. Some players more clearly and practically focused on diagnostic tests, such as providing not just genomics data, like markers and maps, but creating and delivering actual products for hospitals and labs to use to detect, prevent, and treat disease. Many others chose to embark on the difficult, time-consuming, and expensive path of discovering and developing new drugs.

To create and capture the value of their inventions, the pure IP plays that the genomics companies initially represented were transformed to look more like the old, traditional pharmaceutical companies that supposedly had been passé. Even the shining stars of the genomics revolution conceded that, although raw IP is essential, discovering, developing, and delivering real products is what is commercially valuable. For example, Celera Genomics concluded that it simply could not generate substantial enough revenue from genomics alone; a big enough market just didn't exist. Instead, Celera Genomics realigned itself to bet the entire company on drug discovery and development. The company brought in experienced management and technical talent from old-line, Big Pharma companies such as Roche and DuPont to help it make the shift. Many smaller players followed, in an often-repeated pattern of shifting strategies and science, new management, and market focus. They would struggle to become "real" companies, not simply virtual, knowledge-based, pure IP licensors.

The decision of these genomics firms to focus on building more integrated, product-based businesses does not at all suggest that the knowledge they generated was worth little. In fact, in a larger intangible and societal sense, many of their scientific discoveries were truly invaluable. But, in a hard-nosed, revenue-generating sense, there often are considerable limitations to what raw IP can produce. Raw IP typically has limited commercial value and only a small, niche market. Customers pay richly for solutions, not abstractions. Even the most prolific generators of basic scientific and technical progress struggle with these unavoidable facts.

If You're So Smart, Why Aren't You Rich?

The world's research universities have long been a wellspring of new scientific and technical knowledge and novel, path-breaking inventions. Their experiences also hold valuable lessons about the uses and limits of IP-focused innovation models. University contributions have been essential in advancing innovations of all kinds, from computing and communications to medicine and the life sciences.

Indeed, according to the National Science Foundation, universities fund more than half of all basic research in the U.S. In recent years, their mission has expanded beyond pure, basic research.

Much like their for-profit counterparts, academic research institutions caught the lucrative IP licensing fever. They founded and funded increasingly larger, more formal, and more sophisticated IP management units and technology transfer programs. Spurred in part by the Bayh-Dole Act of 1980, which pushed the commercialization of federally supported academic research, American universities were quickly in the lead in this IP commercialization race, far ahead of their Canadian and European counterparts. Membership in the Association of University Technology Managers (AUTM) reflected this booming interest. AUTM membership grew more than three-fold in just a decade, from 1,015 in 1993 to 3,200 by 2003. Increased patenting and increased patent licensing was the first focus and priority of these IP commercialization efforts.

Without a doubt, university IP licensing has grown to be a lucrative side business, at least for a handful of elite institutions. But, even among this elite, a glance at the actual numbers is revealing. Take the most elite of the elite research universities. In 2002, the Massachusetts Institute of Technology (MIT) generated a total of $26 million in gross IP licensing revenues. This is certainly a lucrative incremental revenue stream, but hardly huge for an institution of MIT's size, history, and brainpower. Stanford University's gross licensing receipts ($50 million) almost doubled MITs. Yet, they still constituted less than 2 percent of Stanford's overall revenues. In comparison, Stanford received $247 million just in NIH grants alone that year. The direct returns to research universities' enormous investments in IP are small, however greatly these discoveries contribute in a larger sense.

The limited size of Stanford and MIT's IP licensing revenue was not because they were new to the game. Neither institution was a novice at technology transfer and IP commercialization. They were already two of the long-established and recognized leaders. Viewed against their total annual R&D expenditures and their total revenue bases, IP licensing for even the most elite and successful academic research institutions is a high gross-margin, but still marginal, contribution. Whether good or bad, the fact is that college sports generates plenty more cash for most schools than does cutting-edge IP.

Limitations of the IP-Centric Model

There are several reasons why even these elite IP generators realize limited royalties from their considerable R&D investments. Some of this is undoubtedly because of the fact that they are, of course, non-profit institutions whose main mission is not to make money. In addition, the phenomena of university IP management and technology transfer remain relatively novel concepts, still in their infancy. As with the genomics companies, however, the primary reason for their limited revenues is simply the nature of basic science and raw IP. Basic science is about generating fundamental knowledge, not selling products; it's about generating new discovery, not discovering huge new revenue streams. However much things have changed during the past decade, the university mission still centers around basic research, with some (and increasing) focus on development, but much less on commercialization. Much of research universities' discovery remains in commercial infancy, undeveloped or underdeveloped. It is quite fitting that these world-class generators of scientific and technical knowledge are non-profit organizations, not for-profit companies.

Only a small share of university-generated patents yield significant commercial interest. Of those that do, only a few generate notable returns. For many universities, licensing returns are so meager that IP management costs (for example, running technology transfer offices) exceed revenues. Overall, university IP licensing revenues are based on a relatively small handful of major universities and on a relatively small handful of blockbuster license agreements. Most of this is even more narrowly focused in the life sciences. Universities' massive R&D investments and their prolific spawn of knowledge and invention are invaluable contributions to innovation. Through direct technology transfer mechanisms and through spillovers, university R&D output offers great public benefit and great commercial potential. However, it does not easily translate into quick, large, and direct financial returns.

No matter how promising a technology might seem, for example, often, no licensee can easily be found. This is one reason why spinouts have become an increasingly popular option that many university technology commercialization offices pursue. Spinouts involve forming a real company to push the IP closer to commercialization and thereby demonstrate and realize more value as it grows. A patent itself is just a kernel. Spinouts offer the possibility to further develop and "scale up" the IP, giving it greater value as this process progresses. But, again, this requires building a "real" company.

Size Matters: Scaling Intellectual Property

The process of commercialization is where most innovation value is added. Raw IP remains a critical ingredient or a cornerstone, but it is not even the entire recipe or a whole blueprint, much less a finished product. It is just a beginning, not the end. Raw IP is the start of a process where value is added in ever-larger, non-linear increments at each stage.

Customers are willing to pay premium prices for finished products that provide real solutions for real problems in the here and now. Customers are willing to pay little or nothing for virtual, abstract ideas and inventions that have uncertain value at best.

Developing these raw ideas takes a tremendous amount of additional time, risk, and investment. In most cases, as innovation goes all the way through the value chain, from raw IP to full commercialization, its relative gross margins might shrink, but its absolute gross margins grow much larger. Pure, raw IP-based business models, therefore, can often be quite profitable in one sense (for example, gross margins). But, they concomitantly might be quite limited in scale, in terms of both absolute revenue and absolute profit potential.

Why does scale matter? For startups, scalability is a serious limiting factor. The level and nature of startup investments and valuation are critically predicated on certain assumptions about market size and the corresponding revenue and profit potential. If these assumptions are way off the mark, it might be difficult for true economic profit to ever be realized. The genomics companies provide many ready examples. This is why most abandoned their original pure IP-centered models.

A decade after its founding, for example, genomics leader Human Genome Sciences generated less than $5 million in 2002 revenues. The other leader, Celera Genomics, did better. Celera boasted fiscal 2003 revenues totaling $88 million. But even that annual tally was worth just about 1 percent of Pfizer's yearly R&D budget or about two days of sales of Pfizer's Lipitor anti-cholesterol drug. These figures help illustrate how raw IP by itself has inherent scale limitations. This is exactly why Celera radically transformed itself from trying to be a generator, repository, and provider of IP into a nascent drug discovery and development firm (a "real" pharmaceutical company). Real drugs are where the real money is.

Here's another perspective. A successful $20 million licensing business with high gross margins seems lucrative in the abstract. Taken into context, however, there is often considerable accounting ambiguity in such calculations; for example, if the firm spends $100 million per year on R&D, is any of that expensed to the portfolio of out-licensed IP? Regardless of such important accounting issues, the bottom line is that even a lucrative $20 million licensing operation is likely to have modest impact at best, either to turbocharge an already successful company or rescue a floundering company, with $1 billion or more in sales. Yet, this is approximately the relative scale of IP licensing revenues for an exemplar like IBM.

IP as a Beginning, Not the End

The case of medical imaging startup PointDx clearly illustrates well the indispensable use, but also the inherent limitations, of IP licensing as a core innovation strategy. PointDX's initial endowment of IP helped give it a strong start and some considerable staying power. Even with these early advantages, PointDX still faced the larger challenge of building a company that could help fundamentally transform the practice of radiology.

David Vining had worked as an academic researcher for more than a decade before founding and leading PointDX. In concert with his former university employer, Vining held some of the key patents related to virtual 3D medical imaging. His patented discoveries made possible non-invasive diagnostic techniques to reduce or eliminate the need for more complicated and invasive procedures. During the 1990s, for example, colonoscopy had become an increasingly common procedure to screen for colon cancer and other conditions. Rather than submitting to a dreaded and uncomfortable colonoscopy, however, patients instead might be able to opt for a non-invasive "virtual" colonoscopy. Doctors could get detailed 3D pictures of organs and tissues from the outside without having to prod and probe from the inside.

Virtual colonoscopy itself was a great invention. But Vining had a much larger vision for PointDX. In the process of developing his patented technologies, he realized that the entire practice of radiology was ripe for change. Using recent imaging and computing advances, there was a fantastic opportunity to transform the process from start to finish. Even by the year 2000, much of the process of radiology differed little from its nineteenth-century roots, when doctors first tried to make sense of blurry X-ray films. The basic science and applied "picture-taking" technology had fantastically advanced in some regards (for example, CAT scans and MRIs), but radiology still remained an idiosyncratic and labor-intensive process. Images had to be captured and then developed. Doctors would read the images and dictate their diagnoses. Dictation needed to be transferred and transcribed. Eventually, all the records would get stuck in a folder and (hopefully) appropriately circulated and stored somewhere for later retrieval or transfer.

PointDX sought to digitize and standardize the process from start to finish. With PointDX's systems, doctors would directly interpret digitized onscreen images by using simple and quick point-and-click interfaces and standard, structured diagnostic codes. The radiology value chain would be greatly simplified and compressed. PointDX's type of system promised to eliminate the slow, laborious, and sequential process of imaging, interpretation, diagnosis, dictation, transcription, verification, and feedback. With instant, real-time technology, all the stages of this process instead could be wrapped into one.

The concept promised to significantly reduce diagnostic costs, delays, and errors; more importantly, it promised to speed and improve diagnoses. Images could be shared instantaneously and simultaneously from any number of locations worldwide, allowing for remote or joint interpretation. Text, numerical, and image databases could be automatically constructed and rapidly mined. This sort of rich data mine would foster research and discovery in a way already common to many other medical and other scientific fields, but still novel for radiology.

Despite such a compelling value proposition, transforming the practice of radiology was a daunting task for a small startup. Moreover, in the wake of the technology bubble bursting, funding sources withered. Where would PointDX get cash for development?

Just as importantly, how would PointDX be able to successfully deal with health-care giants who might also have interests in, or even designs on, this new market space? For years, General Electric and other medical imaging leaders had already continued to ignore PointDX's existing patent infringement claims.

PointDX pressed on and enlisted help. In the late 1990s, after years of litigation, imaging equipment maker Fonar finally won a $100 million patent-infringement judgment against GE Medical Systems and had settled with other manufacturers. PointDX took notice of the case and retained the services of Fonar's IP counsel. GE and company finally began to pay attention.

By 2003, PointDX settled for agreements awarding it modest though significant patent royalties from GE, Siemens, and Philips. As a result, through this process, PointDX was able to circumvent the more traditional and often onerous venture capital process and yet still proceed to fund development of its larger business plan by using the royalty stream from its basic imaging patents. CEO Vining could have simply cashed out on these royalties and claimed victory. But, however rewarding, patent royalties alone were not nearly enough to build a substantial and sustainable company.

PointDX cleverly and aggressively used its IP to give it development cash and to buy it some time and breathing room. It got the attention of, and helped ink deals with, the biggest global players in medical imaging. PointDX then could more fully concentrate on its core innovation. It could focus on getting product developed and out the door, and on convincing doctors and health care providers to change their deeply entrenched ways.

PointDX's IP licensing tactics did not eliminate its core innovation challenges or eliminate the inherent risk of being a startup. However, at least they helped give the company a chance at a promising new market—a chance it probably otherwise would not have had. PointDX tactically used its fundamental patents to fund and support its larger, longer-term R&D and business development strategy. In turn, by crafting a more comprehensive suite of functions and products that promised to radically simplify and yet increase the power and capabilities of the radiology value chain, PointDX made itself an attractive acquisition candidate for the big players in biomedical equipment and services.

Turning Licensing Inside-Out

With the growth of IP licensing, it's necessary to take a look at this equation from the perspective of the licensee. Out-licensing's more homely twin, in-licensing, received less attention and consideration from innovation enthusiasts. Few have focused their attention on the licensee because the glory and the gains of royalties flow more to the innovative licensor. This one-sided focus is unfortunate because in- and out-licensing are two sides of the same coin. For every licensor, there is obviously at least one licensee (and often many more). The fact is that, for many firms, in-licensing will play a more important role in their core innovation strategies than out-licensing. In more and more situations, successful and profitable innovation commercialization depends more on in-licensing skills and capabilities rather than out-licensing activities.

The two primary drivers of a change in attitudes toward in-licensing are, first, the explosion of technological complexity and, second, rapidly rising economies of scale and scope. With the rise of technological complexity of all kinds of products and services, no company could do everything by itself. All the individual pieces, and all the technology to tie it together, were too much for one company to handle. During the 1990s, in-licensing a bit here and a bit there grew to constitute more of a growing panoply of complex finished products and services. IBM's licensing success was, in large part, driven by this phenomenon.

The Core Role of In-Licensing

RF Micro Devices provides a good example of both the foundational importance of a fundamental kernel of raw IP, but also of the critical and complementary importance of in-licensing. Analog Devices, long a leading semiconductor firm, was going through tough times in 1991. Bill Pratt was one of the engineers the company let go that year. As part of his severance package, Pratt wrangled the rights to some novel IP that he had generated. He had been doing experimental research on a new material, gallium arsenide, to make chips for wireless applications. Pratt used these discoveries to found RF Micro Devices. It was cutting-edge stuff, but a bit too cutting edge. To Analog Devices, it seemed untested, uncertain, and infeasible; the company was happy to let Pratt have it.

Analog Devices was right. Pratt and RF Micro Devices co-founders Jerry Neal and Powell Seymour struggled for years to get the technology to work, but it simply would not cooperate. Defense and aerospace company TRW had something that might help, however. TRW had developed a different, but related technology that it had been using to produce small quantities of chips for satellite communications. In conjunction with RF Micro Devices's technology, the resulting product was simpler and better—it actually worked as advertised. TRW, however, had no particular focus or interest in the wireless market. So, in exchange for in-licensing the technology, RF Micro Devices gave TRW nearly one-third of its equity. It was a steep price, but RF Micro Devices might have failed without the deal. The technology was essential.

RF Micro Devices's experience highlights how licensing inherently entails the sharing of innovation's value. Whoever has the stronger bargaining position, the more rare and essential assets needed to bring an innovation fully to market, can command more of the gains. Sometimes, the licensor is in the stronger position to capture most of the value, and sometimes, the licensee is in the stronger position. This is an inescapable fact, and one of the key strategic and financial caveats of relying on either out-licensing or in-licensing for innovation commercialization. Armed with TRW's in-licensed technology, RF Micro Devices powered forward with its gallium arsenide breakthroughs and went on to become a global leader in wireless communications chips. Needless to say, TRW earned a good return on its investment as well, cashing out a healthy gain when it sold its equity stake. For RF Micro Devices, in-licensing was the critical key it needed to unlock the value of the innovation it had been working on for years, but could not fully bring to fruition by itself.

The Ins and Outs of In-Licensing

Along with the rise of technological complexity, economies of scale and scope in many industries also soared during the past decade and worked to push the in-licensing trend even further. Increases in scale and scope were not just in R&D, but also in manufacturing and marketing. Bigger scale and scope meant the need for more technology and product to spread out over huge fixed investments. In-licensing offered a ready source. After years of expansion, for example, Big Pharma reached limits to its R&D productivity and desperately needed more drugs to sell through global sales and marketing organizations that had grown ever-larger and more expensive to maintain. In-licensing innovation promised a quick way to fill product pipelines that had been drying up or to otherwise plug holes in their product portfolios.

As important as in-licensing has become, the in-licensing trend itself has sometimes been promoted by questionable assumptions. These assumptions posit in-licensing as not just a compromise, but actually a preferred solution to innovation deficiencies. Don't fret about the lack of productivity of your own R&D labs. Fill the gaps by paying for innovation on the open market through in-licensing deals.

In-licensing is not without risks and costs, however. Just as with any other innovation investments, you get what you pay for. Raw, early stage IP is relatively cheap to license. It also is less proven, more risky, and will take much more time and cash to develop to full commercialization, assuming it does not fail in the process. Later-stage, more fully developed IP (near the actual product stage) might be much less uncertain and feel safer to in-license, but it almost certainly will be exponentially more expensive.

Two of the leading large pharmaceutical companies, Merck and Bristol-Myers Squibb, provide good illustrations of the upsides and downsides of both in-licensing approaches. Merck decided to bet on earlier stage technology by in-licensing a new diabetes drug candidate from Kyorin Pharmaceutical of Japan. The price for the deal was reasonable, but (or, more precisely, because) the compound had not yet been tested in humans. After closing the deal, a troubling longer term assessment of the drug's animal trials came back and Merck suddenly halted human testing. The surprise news dealt a public blow to Merck in the wake of a few other, similarly disappointing announcements just a few months earlier. Earlier stage in-licensing offers greater opportunity at lower cost. But it almost necessarily entails greater uncertainty and risk, and requires much greater additional investment and toil to develop.

Bristol-Myers Squibb seemed to face much less uncertainty when it inked a deal with biotechnology firm ImClone. The September 2001 deal was to license ImClone's revolutionary new cancer drug, Erbitux. By the time of the transaction, Bristol-Myers faced a gnawing shortage of new drugs in its pipeline and patent expirations for some of its key existing products. ImClone's Erbitux seemed a good, safe bet. Based on the positive results of initial trials, the FDA had "fast-tracked" Erbitux and was expected to give final approval shortly. Bristol's own weakened drug pipeline did not put it in the strongest bargaining position, raising the price of the deal. The price tag for such a promising, late-stage drug candidate was quite high.

Bristol-Myers paid $1 billion—a 40 percent premium over ImClone's stock price—for a 19.9 percent stake of the company, plus committed another $1 billion in installment payments. Under the agreement, ImClone would still retain the rights to almost 40 percent of Erbitux's net sales or 60 percent of the profits. This was quite a change from the usual 5–15 percent flat royalties that a typical drug-licensing deal might command. Bristol-Myers's deal included the U.S. market, but only joint rights for Japan; Europe was excluded because rights had already been licensed to another firm.

Bristol-Myers's agreement was a blockbuster deal, but mostly for ImClone. For its part, ImClone's rich deal represented the value of more than 15 years of expensive and extensive R&D behind Erbitux and huge market potential ahead of it, as it was just on the cusp of final FDA approval. ImClone was licensing a valuable, nearly finished product, not just raw IP. Even this late-stage deal was not entirely without risk, however. In December 2001, the FDA surprised Bristol-Myers by refusing to let Erbitux move forward, citing the need for ImClone to provide more and better clinical data. Bristol-Myers was caught in the downdraft. The sustained, hard slide in its share price reflected not just this single piece of disappointing ImClone news, but it also reflected skittishness at how dependent Bristol-Myers had become on such expensive and lopsided licensing deals. In-licensing is not without considerable costs and risks under even the best conditions.

The Ambiguity of Intangibles

IP licensing carries other risks and costs as a model for either sourcing or commercializing innovation. These risks and costs are not at all a reason to shun the strategy, but they are reason to proceed with proper due diligence. Ultimately, licensing is a legal agreement between two parties regarding property rights. Ownership and control of such intangible property can be slippery concepts; licensing rights are subject to interpretation and dispute. What geographic territory is covered by the licensing agreement: U.S., Europe, Japan, the world? For what specific application (for example, for what specific product or use)? In what specific shape, form, or formulation? Does the licensing agreement cover just a basic drug, for example, or does it also include derivatives such as extended-release and prolonged-action versions of the drug?

These might seem like trivial issues, but they're not. They can result in disputes with multibillion-dollar implications. The drawn-out battle between Amgen and Johnson & Johnson over their co-developed anemia drugs is one of the more hotly contested licensing battles. More such battles are a virtual certainty in a wide variety of industries as the New Economy, and the role of IP in it continues to grow and evolve.

In 1985, Johnson & Johnson agreed to acquire the rights to co-develop, manufacture, and market the genetically engineered anemia drug, erythropoietin (Epogen), from biotech startup Amgen. The deal covered U.S. rights to use the drug for general anemia and for all uses in Europe. Amgen retained all domestic marketing rights for kidney dialysis patients. The drug also held enormous promise for alleviating anemia in cancer patients (typically a result of chemotherapy) and other indications. By 1989, just as final FDA approval for Epogen seemed imminent, Chugai Pharmaceutical of Japan starting exporting its own version of erythropoietin, licensed from Genetics Institute in Boston, to the U.S. Amgen locked into fierce legal action in patent disputes with both Genetics Institute and its partners.

What was more curious was the action of Amgen's own licensee, Johnson & Johnson. Unexpectedly, Johnson & Johnson took legal action of its own against Amgen. Johnson & Johnson filed suit to stop Amgen from going to market with Epogen. With Amgen first to market, Johnson & Johnson feared that physicians would begin prescribing Amgen's Epogen "off-label" for various conditions besides kidney dialysis, shrinking Johnson & Johnson's market potential and market share. Johnson & Johnson accused Amgen of purposefully dragging its feet in helping get Johnson & Johnson's identical version of the drug, Procrit, approved and to market.

In turn, Amgen had its own complaint. Amgen discovered that Johnson & Johnson intended to pursue the broader U.S. anti-anemia market, not just for cancer and related conditions. Johnson & Johnson clearly intended to target the renal (kidney) market that Amgen thought it had contractually reserved for itself in its licensing agreement. Amgen had used the term "dialysis" in its agreement with Johnson & Johnson, intending it as shorthand to generally refer to kidney-related disease. Johnson & Johnson saw the agreement differently and more literally. For Johnson & Johnson, everyone except patients actually currently using dialysis was fair game for its version of epo, Procrit. Amgen feared that Johnson & Johnson would hook doctors of early stage (pre-dialysis) renal patients and then keep them in its fold with Procrit, cutting directly into Amgen's own Epogen dialysis-patient market.

Amgen won its suit against Genetics Institute in 1991. However, the battle with its licensing partner, Johnson & Johnson, intensified as Procrit received FDA approval in 1991, 19 months after Epogen itself. Licensor and licensee were now their own chief competitors. During the next few years, Johnson & Johnson prevailed in most of its legal disputes; Amgen was ordered to pay it hundreds of millions as a result. The dispute's intensity was for good reason. Epo quickly became the most successful biotechnology drug ever introduced. Within just a few years of its introduction, it was a billion-dollar plus drug for both Amgen and Johnson & Johnson.

The licensor-licensee battle took on new dimensions by the end of the decade. In 2001, Amgen had a chance to turn the tables on Johnson & Johnson when the FDA approved Amgen's new, long-acting version of erythropoietin, Aranesp. Johnson & Johnson argued that Aranesp was simply a refined version of the original Epogen and therefore was governed by the original licensing agreement. Amgen disagreed, claiming Aranesp was an altered molecule covered by different patents and therefore outside of the original license. Amgen prevailed in arbitration, winning sole rights to Aranesp. This was not an inconsequential issue for Johnson & Johnson; Procrit accounted for about 20 percent of Johnson & Johnson's earnings by 2002. Amgen's Aranesp quickly gained market share and sharply curbed Procrit's sales. Within two years of its launch, Aranesp already was a billion-dollar plus blockbuster for Amgen, with no share for Johnson & Johnson.

Fortunately, the blockbuster success of epo made it mostly a win-win for both parties, despite all the fierce legal, financial, and marketplace battles. Such situations are not always win-win. Even in the most successful deals, licensing presents unique challenges for both licensor and licensee because of the ambiguous and contestable nature of IP itself. These are problems that the outsourcing of innovation through licensing inherently raises for both licensor and licensee.

In-Licensing: Hollowing Out the Core?

Going it alone truly is increasingly less feasible. In-licensing therefore might be necessary in many situations. Over time, however, relying too much on in-licensing to address *core* innovation challenges can be a more and more uncertain, unstable, and unsustainable proposition. In the pharmaceutical industry, for example, by 2003 almost half of the biggest blockbuster drugs were not developed by their Big Pharma marketers and instead were in-licensed or otherwise acquired from outside. This situation led some investors and other observers to ask some serious questions: To what end was all the record-setting R&D investment of Big Pharma in recent years? Despite a tripling of R&D spending to more than $30 billion over the past decade and despite a "fast-track" overhaul of the FDA approval process, by

2003, Big Pharma was bringing new drugs to market in the U.S. at the slowest rate in a decade. This was especially the case for truly new therapies, not just "me, too," copycat drugs. A December 2003 study by Bain claimed that, because of the combination of soaring expenses and declining productivity, the return on investment (ROI) on Big Pharma's internally developed new drugs had plunged to just 5 percent. The ROI of Big Pharma's in-licensed new drugs was not much better, at just 6 percent. In their increasingly desperate bid for new drugs, Big Pharma had pushed up the price of licenses and incurred increased co-development and marketing costs at the same time. For neither internal development nor licensing did it seem that ROI was anywhere near the risk-adjusted cost of capital.

The bottom line is that in-licensing is useful, often critical, as part of a more comprehensive innovation strategy. By itself, however, in-licensing is not a simple, comprehensive solution to the core challenges of innovation. While out-licensing raw IP offers limited value creation and value capture and limited sustainability, over-reliance on in-licensing can lead to the hollowing out of a firm's core innovation capabilities. This, in turn, can lead to an ever-weaker position versus licensors, higher (more desperate) prices for licenses, and ultimately less competitiveness and decreased returns, potentially starting a vicious cycle.

Bottom Line: How Real Is the IP Revolution?

So how real is the virtual revolution of innovation as IP licensing? Is out-licensing IP a workable business model for innovation commercialization or is it an inherently limited strategy? Is aggressive in-licensing a sign of nimble prowess in navigating the technology challenges of the New Economy or is it a sign of R&D weakness, a second-class approach to innovation?

The bottom line is that most of the IP-focused innovation movement is quite real—with a few key caveats. Even most of the richest IP licensing companies continue to generate these returns as derivatives or byproducts of their massive, ongoing core R&D efforts. They have not transformed themselves into purely or even primarily virtual, asset-lite, knowledge-based IP licensors. Although exceptions exist, proactive IP management and IP licensing tools and tactics are critically necessary complements to, but not substitutes for, a more comprehensive core innovation strategy. In the vast majority of cases, a "virtual" strategy—relying solely or primarily on either out-licensing or in-licensing—simply will not allow a firm to either create or capture most of the value from innovation.

Nonetheless, smart IP management is no longer optional; it is a necessity. This is true if only in defense (i.e., the best defense is a good offense). Both private and public investors will shy away from startups or mature firms alike if they do not have their IP portfolios clearly and aggressively ordered and protected. Potential partners will not partner with a firm whose IP assets are of ambiguous defensibility, and customers might shun such firms for more certain and safe suppliers. IP management has become a top management concern, not just a legal issue, and a necessary cost of doing business.

To offset these IP management costs, it makes sense to try to actively generate offsetting revenue from IP as well. If the organization's IP portfolio has sufficient scale and scope, establishing a substantial internal IP management division and staff might make sense as long as the proceeds exceed the costs. Accounting can get complicated in these situations, however, as the firm's operating businesses typically have funded most of the R&D. Much of the enthusiasm for IP licensing neglects these sorts of issues (such as billions and decades of cumulative R&D) and treats IP revenues as if they were just an unexpected windfall rather than returns to considerable investments.

If an organization's IP portfolio lacks scale on its own merits and represents non-core assets, outsourcing much of the footwork might make good sense. An entire industry of advisors and consultants exists specifically for these purposes: Acorn Technologies, InteCap, IPValue, Product Genesis, ThinkFire, and so on. Either fee-based or gain-sharing relationships can be set up to let parent company executives focus on their core businesses while their partners and advisors focus on seeking and closing licensing and other IP commercialization deals. Even larger organizations with great stores of IP have found such assistance to be useful. In 2003, for example, Xerox signed a 5-year agreement with IPValue, making them a worldwide agent for external commercialization of Xerox's IP assets. Such deals can help keep IP management and licensing from becoming an undue distraction that detracts from a firm's core innovation and thereby destroys value overall. Core innovation must be the main game; IP management and licensing need to support, not detract from, this primary goal (see Table 3-1).

Table 3-1 IP and Licensing: A New Model for Innovation?

	The Promise/The Theory	**The Problem/The Reality**
IP Licensing: Out-Licensing	**Strategic Logic** Go more virtual, asset-lite, intangible. Focus on generating and protecting IP: ideas, patents, copyrights, and so on. Outsource the rest: Let others do the laborious, asset-intensive, and mundane tasks of commercialization.	Most added value comes as the commercialization process unfolds, not from raw IP. Holders of critical commercialization assets and capabilities capture most of the profits. "Knowing" requires "doing": getting involved with development and the market, suppliers, customers, and so on.
	Financial Logic "Knowledge is the most valuable asset." IP = monopoly profits. Highly leveraged gains. Rich margins.	Raw knowledge and undeveloped IP have very limited value. Gross margins might be high, but revenue is limited to small niche markets. High legal/policy risk for IP value. Curious accounting for IP profits often ignores years of R&D and billions invested, treats IP as if it materialized from nothing.

(continued)

Table 3-1 IP and Licensing: A New Model for Innovation? (*continued*)

	The Promise/The Theory	The Problem/The Reality
	The Paradigm A new model for capturing the value from innovation.	Limited value creation and capture by itself; limited scale and sustainability. IP is as much a byproduct of innovation success, not necessarily the source of it. A critical complement to, but not a substitute for, a more comprehensive and core innovation strategy.
IP Licensing: **In-Licensing**	**Strategic Logic** Outsource R&D, ideas, and patents. Get key IP quickly and readily from others. Fill holes in complex technology needs and product lines.	Hollowing out of core innovation capabilities. Increasing dependence and desperation for others to develop key innovations—if they ever develop them at all. Loss of competitive advantage and profitability.
	Financial Logic Makes smart financial sense: Let others take the risk and then just license it. Avoid own massive and risky R&D investments. A financial win-win for licensor and licensee.	You get what you pay for: Early stage IP is cheap but risky, and it requires more money to develop; late-stage IP less risky, but prepare to pay handsomely for it. "Everybody's doing it": bidding wars for in-licenses and depressed profitability. Licensor-licensee disputes over cut of rights, markets, and profits.
	The Paradigm A new model for sourcing innovation.	A critical complement to a core innovation strategy but with definite risks and costs if it's relied on too much.

The Future of Innovation as IP Licensing

Beyond the caveats previously discussed, the future of an IP-centric model remains unclear in many ways. The increasing rapidity of technological progress means that technology lifecycles continue to be compressed, making a 20-year patent commercially valuable for as little as just a few years. New technologies and patents might leapfrog old ones even before R&D costs are recouped. The business of "inventing around" and otherwise (quite legally) mimicking IP also continues to flourish. Even a good patent is no longer necessarily much of an effective monopoly. Pfizer's Viagra was a successful new product, for example, but it did not take long before the introduction of Levitra and Cialis seriously slashed into its market share.

Moreover, the concept and future of IP itself remains in flux. This is not a trivial issue for an IP-only innovation strategy. All the profits from IP flow solely from governments' willing recognition and enforcement of patents as officially sanctioned monopolies. The trend is not unidimensionally for increasing IP protection. In many cases, the trend actually is toward considering weakening such restrictions.[8] Even some ideological free marketeers note that a "patent-anything-and-everything" mania threatens to stifle innovation more than foster it and otherwise harm the public good. Courts, regulators, and legislatures have not been deaf to such concerns, whether in regard to software, creative content, or medicine.

In most of the world outside the U.S., for example, IP protection has tended to grow and strengthen. However, it still remains relatively weak and varied. Emerging markets remain huge consumers of U.S. firms' IP, although most of it nets the IP "owners" little or nothing. Europe hesitates to endorse software patents, much less the rest of the world recognizing and enforcing U.S. companies' patents on the human genome. Poorer countries continue to feel a right and an imperative, for both social and economic reasons, for more lax or varied IP protections. Ill citizens earning $500 or even $5,000 per year, for example, cannot afford $5,000 or $15,000 worth of patented HIV drugs annually. U.S. IP standards and practices are not the only ones, and no predestination states that they will prevail globally. Both domestically and abroad, more public and private stakeholders resist high "tolls" companies charge for patents that, of course, are granted and enforced at the discretion of their governments in the first place.

In an increasingly global economy, these issues cannot be ignored. The more a company pursues an IP-centered innovation model, the more the outcomes of these legal and policy debates will outright determine company success or failure. The policy and legal risks for IP-centric firms are enormous, with the very real possibility of abrupt, value-vaporizing downsides. Genomics stocks reeled in early 2000, for example, after Bill Clinton and Tony Blair's offhand observations about the need to freely disseminate to humanity the decoded human genome data.

Regardless of these persistent uncertainties and unforeseen changes, IP has assumed greater importance in the New Economy now and for the foreseeable future. The intangible, knowledge-based content of the U.S. and global economies will continue to increase. Technological complexity and economies of scale and scope will continue to push companies to more actively license (both in- and out-license). Smart and aggressive IP management strategies will be essential for helping capture more of innovation's value. In this sense, the enthusiasts for an IP-centered model of innovation had a very real case, even if sometimes overstated. This new approach is only part of a continuing evolution, however, not a revolution. For most firms, IP licensing will remain a critical part of a more comprehensive innovation strategy, not an entirely new innovation model on its own.

4

INNOVATION BY ALLIANCE
Reconsidering Innovation Collaboration

"[T]here have been dozens of consortiums that have come and gone in the past 30 years and there isn't a single one that has been successful."

—Palm Inc. Executive

Licensing wasn't the only way to expand the boundaries of innovation. For many R&D and commercialization purposes, alliances seemed a more promising and less passive option. Accordingly, the concept and practice of innovation collaboration expanded dramatically during the past decade. Alliances were offered as a solution to a host of emerging innovation challenges.[1] Basic research partnerships, as well as many other types of development-stage joint ventures and more encompassing and elaborate consortia, all grew in number and size.

At least three things were different about this innovation-by-alliance trend compared to the more established and traditional joint venture approach. First, collaboration increasingly became viewed as a critical way to accomplish more—and more basic—R&D tasks, as opposed to just later-stage commercialization such as manufacturing or marketing. Second, innovation alliances increasingly involved more and more collaborators—not just two JV partners—including complex mixes of private, public, and non-profit organizations. Related, and perhaps the most novel, was the New Economy notion that innovation by alliance was an increasingly essential strategy to succeed in the emerging "networked" economy.[2] The idea was that innovative firms in many sectors (especially high technology) no longer succeeded primarily on their own merits. Instead, innovators flourished or failed more and more as a function of the success of their alliance "webs," "networks," or "ecosystems," depending on the particular metaphor used.

The Perils of Partnering

As with most of the other innovation fads and fashions, there was more than a little substance behind the hype. But, much of the rush to find partners ignored the fact that, although alliances play an important role in the innovation mix, they have many limitations and drawbacks. They are intuitively appealing in the abstract, but have a much weaker and more complicated record in practice.

Whatever their benefits, innovation alliances involve a series of compromises and complexities that more tightly unified, integrated, and coordinated innovation approaches simply do not confront. Partnerships can impede quick and effective decision-making. They can be stunningly slow, inefficient, unfocused, and quarrelsome.

Rather than help, alliances can actually impede development and commercialization. From Airbus to Sematech, Corning to Fuji Xerox, General Magic to Iridium and Symbian, some of the most celebrated examples of innovation collaboration have a mixed record at best.

Moreover, the role of some of the most important types of "new" innovation alliances often is not to give any particular firms competitive advantage or superior profitability. Instead, the goal is to help set a common context (for example, to create a "community" or set standards) for all stakeholders in a given new technology or market. Such collaboration might be necessary, but it is far from sufficient, for commercial success. Even when effective, most of the benefits of such open alliances usually go to customers or other stakeholders. They tend to produce great "public goods," not necessarily high private profits. Paradoxically, even as many network or ecosystem alliances flourish, companies are likely to watch rivalry intensify and profits wither.

Finally, whatever their usefulness, R&D partnerships and other forms of alliances cannot substitute for a firm's core innovation needs. Indeed, too much emphasis and investment in external collaboration can distract and detract from a more critical focus on core innovation. In a large number and wide variety of the cases we examined, this was an unfortunate byproduct of the alliance itself—regardless of its success (or, more often, failure). At their best, innovation alliances typically serve as a critical complement to core innovation, not as an alternative solution.

Collaboration Comes in Many Forms

The topic of innovation by alliance encompasses many different forms and functions, so the topic is difficult to quickly summarize or easily generalize. This section, therefore, focuses on the most important dimensions of innovation collaboration, including its most important uses and limitations in practice. Innovation alliances generally take one of these three forms:

- Strategic alliances directly between two partners, typically focused on specific research, development, and/or commercialization objectives

- Independent joint ventures or multiple-partner consortia, formally established as separate entities with their own charter and agendas

- Looser and more open consortia or "network" alliances, often involving a large number and wide variety of private, public, and non-profit collaborators

With so many options and so many potential players, innovation by alliance can quickly become a complicated mix.

Collaborating to Compete

What motivated the increasingly urgent rush to find innovation partners? During the past decade, innovation alliances grew in number and variety for several key reasons. The changing nature of technology itself was a powerful driver of greater emphasis on innovation collaboration. Increasing technological complexity meant that no one firm could quickly and completely put together all the myriad pieces of a new product or service by itself. All kinds of newfangled hardware needed software, for example, and vice versa. Even the biggest firms needed assistance; they needed partners to help put all the pieces together into a workable (and marketable) package. In this sense, some of the same fundamental forces that pushed the growth of in-licensing and innovation by acquisition—such as technological complexity and time pressures—also pushed the trend toward more numerous and diverse innovation alliances.

In a similar fashion, soaring technological economies of scale (in R&D, manufacturing, and marketing) meant that larger required investments more frequently stretched any individual firm's resources, even industry leaders. The semiconductor industry exemplified this trend, as the necessary scale of chip-manufacturing foundries grew into the multiple billions of dollars per facility. Beyond the imposing scale of such investments, the more rapid and radical nature of technology shifts meant greater uncertainty and risk. Fewer firms were willing and able to take on the full share of such huge investment risks by themselves. Not only were the bets bigger, but the odds felt worse. Safety in numbers appeared to be a better gamble.

Under such challenging conditions, many firms found the potential benefits of innovation alliances irresistible. Innovation collaboration allowed two or more players to share the costs and split the risks. Two or more players could "synergize" and bring together their complementary strengths without having to unnecessarily waste money on duplicated and competing R&D efforts. Technology standards could be more quickly created and broadly established, greatly reducing uncertainty and rapidly expanding the entire market for new products and services. Innovation alliances brought together greater combined scale and strength, and more resources and capabilities than any one firm alone could hope to muster. All the partners could prosper. Intuitively, it just seemed to make sense.

Global Alliance Games

Along with these factors, globalization itself pressured domestic competitors to band together against perceived foreign foes. Governments began to encourage R&D collusion among competitors; even longstanding antitrust policies in the U.S. and Europe were waived. Policy makers gave their blessing and sometimes even direct financial support for these national "pride and protectionism" technology alliances. Sematech, for example, was founded and funded as a U.S.-centered industry/academic/government consortium that focused on developing cutting-edge semiconductor technologies. Sematech's goal was to help U.S. companies respond to what was perceived to be an immense threat from the rapid rise of the Japanese semiconductor industry in the late 1980s and early 1990s.

Europe and Japan founded and funded a series of their own R&D consortia and even more extensive, fully developed innovation alliances. The pan-European Airbus consortium was one of the most successful examples. It had been formally founded many years earlier, but really took off in the 1990s. By the end of the decade, Airbus was not only the pioneer of numerous new aviation technologies, it also helped push U.S. firms Lockheed and McDonnell-Douglas out of the commercial aircraft business altogether. Airbus was aggressively innovating technologically and, in the marketplace, competed head-to-head with (if not besting) Boeing. With bold initiatives, such as the Super Jumbo aircraft, some even perceived Airbus as taking the lead. Boeing scrambled to keep pace.

Complex Lessons of Innovation Alliances

In a longer historical sense, innovation alliances were not entirely new by any means. Both R&D and commercialization joint ventures had a long and solid history that extends far before the recent wave of innovation mania peaked. A handful of historical examples had become quintessential success stories used to promote the great potential of innovation collaboration. Besides Sematech and Airbus, Corning and Fuji Xerox were two of the most prominent alliance exemplars.

During its long history, for example, Corning had repeatedly partnered its glass-working R&D and manufacturing expertise with numerous other companies. Corning founded a series of joint ventures, many of which became successful standalone companies such as Owens Corning and Dow Corning. Another classic and much cited example of innovation collaboration was Xerox's joint venture with Fuji Photo Film. Fuji Xerox evolved (even if largely unintentionally) from a simple Japan-focused manufacturing and marketing joint venture into a broad global alliance that served as a key source of improved technologies, products, and processes for its parent, Xerox. During the 1980s, Fuji Xerox's contributions helped generate higher quality and lower cost copiers and printers that allowed Xerox to compete more effectively with new and aggressive Japanese competitors.

However, in an often repeated pattern, even as the fashion for more and greater innovation alliances began to gather momentum, the exemplars of innovation collaboration already were seriously reconsidering their own strategies. Changing business and industry conditions, especially fast and focused new competitors, had rapidly altered the sense of their alliances. What had previously seemed like unassailable alliance advantages turned into handicaps and liabilities. Few seemed to notice or pay heed to these exemplars as they turned into glaring counterexamples.

As the 1990s drew on, Corning drastically simplified its widespread web of joint ventures, selling or spinning off multiple such operations in a bid to regain focus. Rather than muddling along as an ever-expanding network of increasingly diversified and scattered alliances, Corning strived to become a more tightly integrated company. The new Corning moved forward with a much more clear concentration on a few select high-technology sectors, such as fiber optics and liquid crystal displays. Its extensive network of alliances was dissolved.

Similarly, by the 1990s, Xerox's global alliance structure with Fuji Xerox and Rank Xerox (Europe) had become a significant hindrance. Xerox had too much duplication of R&D and manufacturing across North America, Asia, and Europe. The complex alliance structure saddled it with internal management squabbles, high costs, and slow product introduction. Xerox bought out and fully consolidated Rank Xerox, but it was too little, too late. By 2000, in a distressed effort to raise cash, Xerox was forced to sell controlling interest in Fuji Xerox to its Japanese partner, Fuji Photo Film, and give up the entire Asia-Pacific market. During all the complicated alliance restructuring, a lean, fast, and tightly focused Canon had supplanted Xerox's global leadership not just in copiers, but also in key growth sectors such as laser printers. Xerox retrenched and refocused on high-end corporate products and services in a bid for survival.

Corning and Xerox were far from alone. At the same time, the strategies of numerous other celebrated innovation alliances also were reconsidered and deconstructed. Despite its notable successes by the end of the 1990s, Airbus continued to struggle with its unwieldy structure of French, German, British, and Spanish partner companies, among others. Its market share success was not always matched by economic performance; its complex organization and inefficient operations remained subsidized in part through direct or indirect support from various interested European governments. To address these shortcomings, Airbus decided to completely reorganize itself from a loose European R&D and manufacturing consortium into a more closely coordinated and tightly unified competitor. Whither the alliance? By 2001, Airbus formally had become a single integrated company.

The experience of the Sematech consortium also offered mixed lessons. The U.S. semiconductor industry did regain global leadership from the Japanese during the 1990s. However, little of this was because of Sematech's direct contributions. Shortly after its founding, in fact, the founders and funders of Sematech realized that it would be too contentious for industry competitors to collaborate on developing new chips and chip technologies. Therefore, Sematech changed its charter to focus almost solely on improving semiconductor manufacturing processes. Meanwhile, following up on their great successes in the 1980s, most Japanese semiconductor leaders continued to heavily bet on further investment in memory chips. This strategy was soon imitated by the likes of other ambitious, up-and-coming Asian technology companies from Korea and Taiwan. Inevitable overcapacity in the memory market led to fierce competition and margin-slashing price wars. Whether by luck or by design, U.S. semiconductor makers had long since abandoned much of this now-commodity memory market; instead, they had switched to the design and manufacture of more complex, higher value-added microprocessors and specialty chips. This was a new "sweet spot" for the chip industry. Sematech's contributions, as much as they might have helped improve chip manufacturing, were clearly not what rekindled the leadership of U.S. semiconductor companies.

Nonetheless, long after their usefulness appeared to wane, these cases continued to be proposed as outstanding models and examples for innovation collaboration. The deeper irony, of course, is that these companies simultaneously were de-emphasizing or abandoning the alliance strategy for their own innovation needs. They already had reconsidered and revamped their own partnering strategies. In most cases, the complexities and difficulties of extensive collaboration had forced them to de-emphasize alliances and to pursue innovation closer to the central cores of their organizations.

Consortium Dysfunctions

Iridium was a shining example of the possibilities of innovation collaboration, one that unfortunately went bust. Much has been written about its ignoble failure. But most retrospectives focused on the *symptoms* of the failure instead of the root *causes*. At its heart, the Iridium experience illustrates the myriad potential problems of innovation alliances, especially more complex efforts involving multiple partners. In March 2000, even before the U.S. stock-market bubble imploded, few paid attention to the imminent collapse of Iridium's multibillion dollar satellite constellation. Iridium's high-flying global mobile communications dreams literally were set to crash to earth. The managing partner of the joint venture, Motorola, prepared to send 66 gleaming, brand-new satellites down to burn up in the earth's atmosphere. After spending more than $5 billion, Iridium was bankrupt, out of cash and out of time, unable even to pay basic operating costs to keep its satellite network in the sky.

This story began earlier in the decade, when Motorola formally announced the launching of Iridium. Over the next few years, Motorola formed a broad and deep-pocketed consortium to help fund Iridium and to develop both the necessary technologies and rich potential markets in literally every geographical region of the world. The audacious scale of the effort seemed to beg for a massive, ground-breaking global alliance. Iridium's promise was to develop and deploy mobile, handheld communications solutions to business customers who needed and demanded "anywhere, anytime" worldwide service. Using a globe-spanning satellite network, Iridium's handset would work equally well anywhere from Manhattan to Mount Everest. Customers would not be bound to local service providers and areas. They would not have to carry multiple phones to accommodate different country standards and service-provider technologies. There would be no frustrating and unpredictable service interruptions and no more "no signal" messages as they traveled around the world. Instead, customers would get seamless global service.

With Motorola as the lead managing partner and most prominent investor, the Iridium consortium took on a long list of other technology and telecommunications leaders as partners: Lockheed Martin, Raytheon, Sprint, Bell Canada, Telecom Italia, and so on. Most of the partners, including Motorola, had a substantial interest in the venture outside of its own success: They either were suppliers of equipment or services or were resellers and marketers to Iridium's end users. It seemed like a win-win for all involved.

Motorola contributed the initial seed capital; technology planning and development proceeded methodically during the next couple of years. However, the major investments came with the actual construction and launch of the satellite network. To meet these immense capital needs, Iridium raised a total of $5 billion. The financing included equity investments from its partners, bank debt, high-yield bonds, vendor financing from equipment suppliers, and the proceeds of a partial $240 million IPO of Iridium World Communications. By 1997, Iridium was ready to launch its satellites and ambitiously announced that it would start service the next year. In an indisputably impressive technical achievement, its satellites were launched and the communications network was rapidly put into place in 1997 and early 1998.

After some embarrassing but relatively minor technical delays, Iridium launched commercial service in late 1998. Despite great fanfare and a massive and expensive marketing campaign to match, the service immediately sputtered. Customers balked at $3,000 phones and astronomical airtime charges of up to $7–9 or more per minute. Even with such a premium price tag, the phones and all the add-on equipment were derided as clunky and cumbersome. The phones did not work well in urban areas or in buildings, which are both serious problems if your key potential customers are traveling business executives. Meanwhile, even as Iridium was being built, tested, and launched, ground-based mobile telephony advanced by leaps and bounds. More mobile competitors were offering greater, increasingly seamless geographical coverage and new, higher quality services at prices lower than ever. Whatever Iridium's serious internal financial, operational, and marketing problems, the rapid technological and competitive evolution of the entire mobile communications sector only exacerbated its difficulties. In August 1999, less than a year after commencing operations, Iridium defaulted on $1.5 billion in loans and filed for bankruptcy.

Requiem for Iridium

Many different analyses of Iridium's failure have been offered. Was it just part of the insane boom and bust of the entire telecom sector? Perhaps in some larger sense. But, the fact is that Iridium's build out, and then its bankruptcy, occurred long before the larger telecom boom even peaked, much less crashed. Most diagnoses have instead focused on the factors previously discussed: high prices, clunky phones, poor service, and so on. The problem with focusing on these factors is that they are *symptoms* rather than root causes.

The root cause of Iridium's difficulties might better be traced to the very nature and structure of the innovation alliance itself. Iridium was a consortium with many inherent conflicts and handicaps. One account noted that Iridium's partner board meetings often seemed like a mini–United Nations gathering, with headsets for translating the proceedings into five different languages.[3] With so many different partners involved, no one party had adequate perspective, sufficient incentive, or enough power to recognize the need for and to make meaningful changes to Iridium's strategy and its implementation at critical junctures. Many specific technical and market concerns were voiced, from both inside and outside, as the venture progressed. However, no single partner had the perspective, incentive, or power to alter the consortium's course until it was too late. Iridium had a momentum all its own. This inertia made it difficult to sense and react to all the warning signals at numerous points along the way.

Making matters worse was that several of the Iridium consortium's key players had conflicting interests, which is typical of so many joint ventures and alliances. Although it was the lead partner and key investor, Motorola's interests and Iridium's interests were frequently not aligned. In Iridium, Motorola had a lucrative and captive customer: It made and sold equipment to the venture under a 5-year, $3.4 billion design-build-launch contract. Curiously, at one point in 1997, Motorola boosted its guarantees of the Iridium consortium's bank loans (to $1.1 billion) so that Iridium could raise the cash it needed to buy satellites from . . . Motorola. Unfortunately, the satellites were far from ideal. They could handle only a relatively small number of calls simultaneously, which greatly limited the network's scalability and dramatically raised its call costs. Motorola also had a multiyear, $3 billion service contract to operate the Iridium network after it was up and running. These high fixed operating costs later became enormous financial baggage for Iridium and a fierce point of contention in its slide toward bankruptcy.[4] Motorola further took the lead on designing and manufacturing the handset equipment it then sold to Iridium. The clunkiness and glitches of its handset equipment quickly gained notoriety.

The bottom line is that, in many joint ventures and alliances, even collaborators with the best intentions can easily become less focused on ensuring the overall success of the partnership and more concerned with carving out their own slice of the pie, even before it's half baked. Motorola's self-dealing contracts with Iridium looked like a logical win-win in the short-term, even for some of the other partners. However, these agreements were a fateful handicap. They severely limited Iridium's strategic options and its financial, technological, and operational flexibility. The Iridium alliance was fatefully handicapped from its inception.

Risk Comes in Many Different Forms

Despite all its travails, Iridium nonetheless could be viewed as a "success" in the sense that it did limit the risks for its participants. For each major partner and investor, especially Motorola, the use of an alliance structure capped the potential losses for any one partner from investing in a bold and risky new idea. This is certainly true in a narrowly defined sense. No one partner had to bear the full force of the multibillion dollar loss when Iridium filed for bankruptcy. On the other hand, this very sense of limited risk enticed both partners and investors to push ahead with a venture that otherwise, quite literally, should never have gotten off the ground. A false sense of safety in numbers—especially because of the blue-chip pedigree of the key collaborators—lured partners and investors to suspend their often well-justified concerns and pour in more cash.

The risk-spreading nature of alliances can lead to collective overconfidence that causes collaborators to push forward with ventures that have questionable business cases and weak risk/reward profiles. The problem is that alliances fundamentally do not eliminate the technological and market risks of innovation. The overall risk remains just as large and real. By parceling it out, however, the risk seems less to all involved, even though the overall odds are no better. In contrast, when a single company has to make more stark and consequential investment choices at each stage of development, it is forced to deal with the total picture of risk. With less perceived threat and with the (false?) confidence of collective clout, Iridium moved forward despite continued doubts and uncertainties about its viability. The partnership had not, in some magical way, reduced or eliminated the real total risk.

Risk is also a multifaceted concept. The real, substantial, longer-term risks of innovation are often less overt and more hidden or subtle. It is true that the financial structure of Iridium limited Motorola's direct losses to only a fraction of the $5 billion invested. Some even claimed that Motorola won from the entire affair despite Iridium's failure because of all the rich contracts and technology Motorola gained from its involvement. Still, although Motorola had just 18 percent of the equity, its complex financial relationship with Iridium made it responsible for more than $2.5 billion in losses and write downs. Banks and bondholders later sued Motorola for $800 million and $3.5 billion, respectively, for its role in Iridium's downfall, though the company got away with paying just a fraction of those claims.

Regardless of these significant and disproportionate direct losses, focusing only on the immediate financial impact misses much of the larger, more important story. The entire Iridium adventure had a more insidious impact. While wrapped in the complexities of developing and launching (and then trying desperately to rescue) Iridium, Motorola made a series of missteps in its core cell-phone business. It dragged and delayed on the switch from analog to digital equipment. It fell behind in introducing new styles and new features. In short, Motorola slipped and then lost its previously unrivaled global leadership in the cell-phone industry. By 1998, the year Iridium was launched, Nokia just narrowly surpassed Motorola in terms of global market share. By 2000, Nokia had twice the global market share of Motorola.

It's difficult to assign precise blame for these strategic stumbles in Motorola's core business. But, its Iridium misadventures were a critical diversion, to say the least. Undue reliance or emphasis on joint ventures and alliances can detract and distract a company from core innovation. The Iridium saga was not just a harbinger of larger problems for Motorola; it indirectly may have been the largest single cause.

Joint ventures and alliances, rather than being quick and synergistic ways to develop and introduce new technologies, products, and services to market, often instead are cumbersome, slow, and rigid. By their very nature and structure, they tend to be conflicted, unresponsive, and inefficient. The potential for problems grows as does the number of players involved. Instead of managing risk better, alliances can actually increase risk taking. By joining together, partners might be lured into a false sense of security as they collaborate to advance ideas with a poor risk/reward profile, ideas that they never would have chosen to pursue individually. Alliances do not get rid of undue risks; they only spread the risk around without bettering the overall odds. The likelihood of failure can actually increase as partner tensions and conflicts arise and as dysfunction and paralysis ensue.

All these points were true in the case of Iridium. Consortium dysfunction was the fundamental cause of its failure. All these issues are especially crippling problems in fast and radically changing industries, as is the case with much of high technology innovation. When considering alternatives, it's important to remember that these are problems not engendered by more tightly unified, integrated, and coordinated approaches to innovation.

The Attraction of Open Innovation Collaboration

Even with many more collaborators, however, more open and inclusive innovation alliances can be surprisingly functional and fruitful because in many ways they offer a lot more flexibility than formal joint ventures or consortia. Rather than build a two-partner or multipartner joint venture, open and networked forms of innovation collaboration involve building a fertile community or ecosystem in which a particular innovation can flourish. Such widespread cooperation has been absolutely essential to advancing R&D and commercialization in a wide variety of technologies and industries: to set standards, to ensure interoperability of hardware and software, even to generate whole new classes of products or services. Through open, active, and enthusiastic collaboration among many different stakeholders, innovation advances and enormous value is created.

The basic logic is that some innovation collaborations make greatest sense with more players in the game. This theory caught on during the innovation boom in various guises: "co-opetition," "positive feedback," "network externalities," and the like. More partners is better; the more players in your "network" or "web," the merrier. The reasoning was that the more allies (especially customers and providers of complementary goods and services, but also even including competitors), the more likely your own offerings would flourish. The bigger and more inclusive the network, the more the entire ecosystem prospers, which creates a rising tide.

The profitability paradox in this expansive and open collaboration model arises from the fact that creating a rising tide for all advantages no single company in the core market. Enormous benefits can be created in a holistic sense. But, unless a specific company somehow has privileged or proprietary control of the playing field, most of the benefits of innovation go to consumers or to providers of complementary goods and services, not to competitors in the core market. In fact, for companies in the core market, free and open collaboration tends to lead to freer and fiercer competition. Rivalry ultimately tends to increase and profits tend to drop considerably. Most created value does not directly flow to the bottom line of any company in the core market; instead, it is captured by other stakeholders.

These types of alliances, therefore, might be a fantastically positive proposition for technology and society as a whole. For profit-seeking innovators, however, the dynamics of such broader collaboration create a serious challenge. There are good, natural reasons why most "standard setters" are organized as non-profit or not-for-profit entities (such as IEEE and ISO). Similarly, it's not just coincidence that some of the most flourishing examples of open and networked innovation collaboration foster relatively modest or meager profits; it's inherent to the form. In recent years, Linux has been the most popular and influential case in point.

Free and Open Software

Like so many other exemplars of innovation, Linux quickly became the stuff of technology legend, even long before it had been established—much less victorious—in the marketplace. Because it was such a compelling story, the excitement and hype predictably outpaced the reality. By the late 1990s, competitors and customers badly craved an alternative to Microsoft's pricey supremacy. Linux was enthusiastically embraced when it first appeared on the scene, even though (in part because) it was a relatively radical and unproven departure from the dominant proprietary software model.

Linus Torvalds was storied as the freethinking founder and original programmer of Linux. In 2000, however, the founding of Open Source Development Labs (OSDL) brought Linux to an entirely new level. The founding members included undisputed technology heavyweights like IBM, HP, Computer Associates, Intel, and NEC; many other leading-technology companies soon joined the bandwagon. OSDL formed as a non-profit organization with the express purpose of supporting and promoting the further development and adoption of Linux.

Never it seemed had Microsoft faced so credible a threat. During the prior decade, Microsoft's grip on the software industry had expanded beyond desktop PC operating systems, to PC applications, to web browsers and the Internet, then to server and enterprise operating systems and applications. Previous attempts to weaken Microsoft's growing domination proved spectacularly unsuccessful as it methodically crushed even much faster, more nimble and innovative, and technologically superior competitors (think Netscape, among many others). Its dominance had grown so thorough that antitrust action against Microsoft seemed many would-be competitors' last resort. They banded together to support U.S. and European action against the company. Even the respective governments' punitive findings against Microsoft proved relatively ineffective at denting its immense power.

Beyond the general craving for any credible (and more affordable) alternative to Microsoft, Linux generated excitement for numerous other reasons. Shareware, open-source, and other such "enlightened" collaboration had long been practice among the tech savvy. The Apache Software Foundation's open-source programs scored a big hit for web servers, for example, quickly capturing a large share of the server market. For broader commercial applications and the mass user market, however, Linux was still a novel concept. It offered threats to Microsoft's software dominance across the board—from the enterprise to the home, from the server to the desktop to the mobile phone.

Linux was not just another company. It was a thriving community. That was precisely its power. It was an open-ended, open-source innovation alliance. That is, unlike Microsoft's proprietary, "secret-source" code, Linux was an open book. Unlike with Microsoft products, Linux users could freely see and explore, alter and improve, the underlying computer code. They could customize and optimize it. In turn, by agreement, users openly shared their inventions and improvements with the larger Linux community.

Linux offered the networked power of a global, non-stop innovation factory, with thousands upon thousands of users and programmers from all over the world sharing in the discovery and the benefits. Linux started to gain traction first in server and enterprise operations, but other applications soon followed. Governments around the world, from Asia to Europe to Latin America, started to openly embrace and promote Linux as an attractive alternative to paying rich tribute to Microsoft, the arrogant U.S.–based software colossus. Beyond its business impact, Linux was a great technological and sociological story, with instant appeal.

Higher Market Share = Lower Profits

In all the excitement, some of the key implications of the Linux movement got lost, at least initially. Looking for a new hot company and the next big thing, entrepreneurs and executives, analysts and investors, paid scant attention to the fact that, even if Linux took off and perhaps even eventually trounced Microsoft, the "next

Microsoft" could never emerge from the Linux movement inherently because of the very nature and structure of the collaboration. Nonetheless, the shares of the leading Linux software and hardware plays, Red Hat and VA Linux, were bid up as if they might actually have a serious shot at being the next Microsoft. In fact, VA Linux set an all-time IPO record with a 700-percent first-day leap in its stock price.

Even at the time, some observers noted the yawning discrepancy between the Linux hype versus the basic economics of the companies' actual business models:

> Linux is the operating-system software that is a growing threat to Microsoft. The many Linux companies that have cropped up in the past few years seem to have a lot going for them. These include marketplace momentum, a loud buzz, and—in the case of Red Hat Software—a multibillion-dollar initial public offering that has numerous other Linux start-ups scrambling to go public, too. There's just one hitch: The Linux operating system can also be had free of charge, downloaded off the Internet.[5]

The business models of the Linux players offered not secret, tightly controlled, and highly profitable software, as did Microsoft. They inherently could not have a monopoly as did Microsoft. Instead, they proposed to make their mark and their money not from the base software but by offering upgrades and add-ons, service and support—or even by making and selling Linux-running hardware.

The excitement over Linux did not die with the deflation of the dot-coms. By 2003, Linux started to become a serious competitor to Microsoft, especially in the server market. And Red Hat remained the dominant name in the Linux world. But the much less lucrative economics of the open-source model, versus Microsoft's proprietary offerings, remained a problem. In January 2004, *Barron's* skeptically noted that continued optimism gave Red Hat a market capitalization of $3.5 billion, which was larger than the entire Linux market. Despite being the leading name in Linux, Red Hat had quarterly revenues of just $33 million and continued to run losses. This compared with revenue of more than $2 billion for Microsoft's "server and tools" division alone. Linux was a great new thing, offered Microsoft its most serious competition in years, and promised even greater innovations ahead. But this would not readily and easily translate into rich profits for its purveyors.

To Linux skeptics, the fact remained that Microsoft reaped its rich profits by avoiding and taking advantage of, not by joining in, the open-architectures and common-standards of the PC industry. After standards emerged, the PC hardware industry itself quickly became one of the most fiercely competitive and thinnest margin businesses, leaving many failed companies in its wake and even causing the standards' originator—IBM—to exit the retail-consumer PC business altogether. Of the major players, soon only Dell managed to eke out a profitable and sustainable position, and only then by being relentlessly hyper-efficient in a bid to combat the inexorable margin squeeze of an industry with ever more commodity-like economics. A similar cycle would soon take hold in many other areas of computing and communications.

Linux won more and more share, especially globally. Compared to the game Microsoft continued to play, however, Linux was a game with dramatically reduced revenue potential and even more shrunken margins. Even if it ended up being an even larger pie overall, most of the value was sliced up and given away to other stakeholders. The model was to charge for service, support, and hardware for core products that nominally were free or low-cost, open-source or standardized. To pursue "razor economics," the concept went: Give the razor away and make a mint on selling the blades. The problem is that the clever-sounding theory and the rich potential of "razor economics" only works well when the blades are *proprietary*. In contrast, Red Hat honestly disclosed:

> Open source software does not mean free as in without cost—but open source does mean that the software is free (as in freedom), meaning no one company can fully own and conceal it. Software lock-in is impossible. . . Will it be as financially lucrative as a software monopoly? No. Will customers more appreciate and realize its value, and therefore become better customers? Absolutely.

The problem is not one of *creating* value. Such open alliances can be fantastically powerful for creating it. Instead, the issue is how to *capture* enough of a share of the value created to devise a workable business model, sustain a company, and earn a decent return on capital. In the aftermath of the initial Linux hype, the companies best poised to capitalize on its success ironically were those who had the strongest ongoing, internal, and proprietary innovation efforts— especially including many established technology hardware, software, and services leaders (such as IBM), but often less so of many of the Linux upstarts.

The Java Community

Sun's Java experience shows how difficult it can be to foster a thriving innovation network, and yet somehow still profit handsomely through a privileged position in that network. In 1995, Sun released Java to much acclaim as alternative (to Microsoft) code upon which to build the software of the future. Java's key attraction was that it was open-source code, freely posted and available for individual use. Adaptation of Java for mass commercial purposes, however, required Sun's approval of any changes and additions; this ostensibly assured the quality and compatibility of all Java programs. Commercial use of Java also required payment of modest (at least in Sun's view) licensing royalties. Despite the initial fanfare, Java got off to a slow start. Users complained about Sun's paternalistic control and its royalty charges.

In response, Sun loosened both. Both Java applets (small, embedded applications) and their developers and users began to multiply. With the explosion of the web and other new applications, such as mobile phones, a substantial Java community emerged. As the Java movement grew, Sun repeatedly squelched rumors that it would jack up its licensing fees to make Java more profitable. Sun publicly re-emphasized its original strategy: to broadly encourage Java development in order to help sell the company's larger hardware and systems. A disconnect existed, however. Nearly a decade after founding Java and despite a flourishing Java community, Sun captured only a small portion of the value created by the innovations it had pioneered, even as it continued to struggle with its core proprietary hardware businesses.

Capturing Value from Open Alliances

As the evolution of Linux and similar innovation alliances show, open and inclusive collaboration can work extremely well for accelerating R&D and fostering wide commercialization. In fact, such alliances are increasingly essential, not optional, as everything literally becomes more networked. Despite being effective for such broader purposes, by its very nature open innovation collaboration does not give competitive advantage or superior profitability to any one collaborator. Broad, diverse, and open innovation alliances therefore may be absolutely essential precursors to building a new technological or market playing field rich with possibilities. But even when these alliances are fantastically successful, by themselves they do not offer a clear path to superior profits for any particular player.

Encouraging open innovation alliances therefore may make good social and public policy. Overall public welfare benefits, even if often at the expense of profitability among competitors in the core market. Customers reap the benefits of many different competitors pushing interoperable and interchangeable products and services, typically with ever-greater features and ever-lower prices. The functionality of the core offering becomes more of a commodity. Prices and profits are pushed down even as volumes increase and ever more value is created.

The bottom line is that open-network alliances do foster innovation and can create enormous "spillover" benefits. Even so, they cannot serve as the centerpiece of a successful *firm-level* innovation strategy. As much as they might want or need to support such extensive collaboration, profit-seeking companies must pursue innovation strategies with their own distinct and proprietary paths to profit. This remains the key challenge, despite the undeniable potential of open network alliances. This is the job of a core innovation strategy.

Of course, having a thriving and expansive but *proprietary* alliance network could offer unparalleled profit potential for the firm that's at the center of it all. But there's obviously no good reason for anyone else to join such a domineered network—unless they're coaxed or coerced, that is. In practice, therefore, these types of "dominant player" webs or ecosystems represent not alliances so much as follow-the-leader supremacy of one central firm typically because of its own extraordinary technological and/or market leadership. An ecosystem grows to enhance and perpetuate this advantage, but the impetus for the thriving network in the first place comes from the dominant firm's powerful core investments in developing and commercializing innovation (such as the frequently used example of Microsoft in software, and any number of other computing and communications leaders, Wal-Mart in retail, and so on). Everyone wants to "partner" with a winner. The dominant firm's technology and market leadership is more often the foundation and focal point of a rich network of partners and other complementors—not the result of it. Overemphasizing the network itself misses this key point and confuses cause with effect.

The Elusive Symbiosis of Innovation Alliances

The story of Symbian showcases the range of different approaches toward innovation alliances: the proprietary approach (Microsoft), the joint venture or consortium approach (Nokia, et al.), and the open-network alliance approach (Linux). Symbian was a consortium formed to provide operating systems and other types of software for mobile phones. It's a case that illustrates well the relative advantages and disadvantages of the different approaches to innovation collaboration that we have discussed so far. Should we go it alone? Should we use joint venture or consortium? Or should we participate in and use an open-network alliance?

As mobile phones grew more complex toward the decade's close, with greater functions and more features, communications and computing began to meld. Mobile phones were trending toward wireless, networked computers: personal digital assistants, web surfers, e-commerce platforms, and more. They would need increasingly sophisticated software to smoothly perform all these functions. They needed powerful but "lite" operating systems. Nokia, Motorola, and a host of other major mobile phone makers had previously performed most of this software work in house. But, with mobile phones morphing into computers, the major manufacturers began to look elsewhere for greater software expertise and solutions.

Microsoft was more than happy to oblige. Having conquered so many other realms, Microsoft made a big push into this new and unconquered territory. The software behemoth began aggressively promoting its own mobile, portable versions of Windows for mobile computing and communications. But, the last thing many of the mobile-phone majors wanted to see was another Microsoft-dominated software monopoly in mobile communications. At first, they resisted. Then, they responded with a powerful alliance.

In June 1998, Symbian was incorporated as an independent company, a for-profit consortium of most of the major mobile phone makers, led by Nokia, and Psion, a U.K.–based leader in mobile computing hardware and software. Ericsson, Matsushita, Motorola, Samsung, Siemens, and others joined in the effort. Each of the major partners was also a major shareholder. All pledged to use Symbian operating systems and software in their next generation of more advanced mobile phones. It was an attractive alternative to being a captive, tribute-paying customer of another Microsoft monopoly.

As a distinct joint venture, Symbian could focus on the software while the mobile-phone makers could continue to focus on their hardware competencies. Together, Symbian's partners represented more than 80 percent of the global handset volume. Their combined efforts would be better, quicker, and stronger; all would gain from the success of the joint venture, from both the software directly and from their equity stakes as it grew. The plan even included hopes for Symbian to perhaps eventually go public. With Psion's software expertise at its core and with so many strong partners involved, the consortium appeared to be off to a great start. Even outside the alliance, many cheered it on. By 2000, the perception was that Symbian was in the lead in developing software for mobile-communications software. Microsoft appeared a weak also-ran, with slow, clunky, and power-hungry offerings.

Despite this strong head start, the nagging fact was that most of Symbian's partners and shareholders remained fierce competitors in the global mobile-handset market. It was an uneasy alliance from the start. Even before Symbian introduced its first product, Nokia was signing separate deals to use software from Palm, the handheld computing leader; Ericsson inked a deal with Microsoft; and other partners openly considered other software options. In mid 2000, one of the key founders and executives of Symbian suddenly left to join Microsoft's mobile software efforts, which lead the consortium to threaten legal action.

Even with this turmoil, Symbian did manage to beat Microsoft to market with its June 2001 software release as part of a new, advanced Nokia phone. But also in 2001, Nokia announced the formation of its own new division, Nokia Mobile Software, to create and license its own mobile software solutions. Meanwhile, Microsoft added a new twist, revealing plans to help foster more standardized and simplified mobile phone architectures to allow new upstart hardware manufacturers to enter the mobile-phone manufacturing game.

Tensions that had been privately bubbling came publicly to the surface as soon as a five-year standstill agreement among Symbian's partners neared expiration. In early 2003, Motorola announced plans for a new advanced phone based on open-source Linux and Java software. Motorola later dumped its entire Symbian stake, left the consortium, and just a few weeks later, announced a new Microsoft Windows–based Smartphone.

Putting the consortium on even more uncertain footing, in early 2004, Psion also sold its entire stake in Symbian. With Nokia as the primary potential buyer, the consortium was poised to become, for good or bad, a de facto Nokia subsidiary. Many observers openly wondered why and whether the other mobile-phone makers who still were part of Symbian would continue to buy operating systems and software from an effective subsidiary of their biggest competitor, Nokia. Why should they not opt for Microsoft or Linux and Java solutions instead? What had seemed to be such a bright future for Symbian was now much in doubt. It was threatened by the unified Microsoft juggernaut on one side and by the relatively free-form, open-source options of Linux and Java on the other side, even as it tried to juggle its own internal consortium discord. On the other hand, at least if Nokia now took more clear and focused leadership of the group, perhaps Symbian might actually have a better chance.

Mobile Computing Redux

To many involved in the computing and communications worlds, Symbian's storyline seems at least vaguely familiar. Wasn't it just a few years earlier that General Magic, the mobile-computing operating systems and software consortium, had garnered even greater excitement and support? In the end, none of its partners were able to use its fruits to succeed in the mobile-computing space. General Magic itself flailed for years and finally folded.

The goal of General Magic and its partners was to come up with the next generation of operating systems and software needed to make mobile computing possible, to take personal computing away from bulky desktops and laptops and make it truly portable. Apple was the genesis of the effort, which began in the early 1990s. However, soon General Magic became one of the most heralded technology consortia in memory, as some of the biggest and best names in communications and computing joined Apple as partners and investors.

Many key names that hopped on the General Magic bandwagon were the same names that, a few years later, were to back Symbian. Motorola, Sony, AT&T, Matsushita, and Phillips were early partners, and other blue-chip names, like NTT, Matsushita, and Toshiba, soon followed. With such powerful backing, General Magic was as close to a sure bet as one could imagine in the risky and uncertain world of high technology. Following this logic, the company even managed to launch a successful IPO in 1995, even though it had no product or revenue yet.

General Magic eventually did launch several versions of its much anticipated software during the next few years. But neither the software nor any of its partners' hardware managed to survive—much less thrive—in the mobile computing marketplace. From Apple's Newton to AT&T's EO to Motorola's Envoy (among others), each failed to gain traction and folded. General Magic itself was left to scramble for a new mission and market. After several years of futile strategic flip-flops, General Magic finally shut its doors. Meanwhile, a more focused and patient Palm, Inc., followed by the methodical and inexorable efforts of Microsoft, gradually took leadership of the mobile computing operating systems and software sector.

Joint Venturing Lessons Learned

The sagas of Iridium, Symbian, and General Magic emphasize the sketchy record of using independent joint ventures or consortia to drive key innovations. No matter how strong the partners, the joint ventures themselves often lack focus and direction. They suffer from inherent tensions and conflicts. They engender dysfunction and paralysis by trying to serve the ends of many different masters, including themselves; in turn, they often end up pleasing no one. They might endure either the neglect or the competitive antagonism of their partners, or both. Joint ventures themselves can even become serious competitors to one or more of their parents, or vice versa.

Sometimes, circumstances make such joint ventures an unavoidable choice. If so, due diligence is essential. They should be carefully structured to align each party's interests and incentives, including those of the joint venture itself. They must have clear objectives and boundaries, including especially vis-à-vis the parents. They must have clear mechanisms for dispute resolution and alteration of the terms of the original joint venture agreement, and clear mechanisms for termination and dissolution after the joint venture outlives its usefulness. Of course, with all these diligent restrictions and well-intentioned limitations in place, it's easy to see why innovation alliances so often fail at their assigned tasks: They tend to be inherently constricted from the get-go.

Joint ventures present inherent tensions and compromises under even the best of circumstances and with the most amiable of partners. They labor under special burdens. Ideally, therefore, the problems of core innovation are best not left in the charge of separate joint ventures or quasi-independent consortia. Nor, ideally, should a core innovation strategy depend on loose and open alliances (see Table 4-1).

With all these caveats, it's important to reiterate that many desirable or necessary but non-core (peripheral or complementary) innovations often *are* best pursued either through dedicated joint ventures or looser, more open alliances. Quite simply, if the needs are non-core, consider an alliance. Open alliances well serve goals such as helping set new standards. Dedicated joint ventures, on the other hand, can be used to help ensure critical supplies and suppliers, necessary but novel manufacturing technologies or production capacity, and so on—especially in the absence of feasible alternative market mechanisms. In the semiconductor industry, for example, the huge scale of chip plants requires manufacturing collaboration among competitors, customers, and suppliers. Also, in the semiconductor industry, the Sematech consortium did help the U.S. semiconductor industry devise complementary advances in manufacturing processes. These types of innovation needs frequently lend themselves to collaborative arrangements rather than internalization. Moreover, joint ventures also can be effectively used as part of a process to spin out and thereby externalize, yet still profit from, non-core innovations (Chapter 6). Using collaboration for such peripheral or complementary tasks can enable a company to keep a keener focus on its own core innovation, even while helping create a more favorable overall context for value creation and capture.

Table 4-1 Innovative Alliances or Joint Problems?

	The Promise/The Theory	The Problem/The Reality
Joint Ventures, Consortia	Bring together complementary resources and capabilities. Synergies, joint learning. Increase speed, strength, clout of innovation. Share innovation costs. Share innovation risks. Reduce risks and potential losses.	Inherent tensions and handicaps built in from the beginning. Conflicts of interest among partners and with joint venture itself. Slow, inertial, hamstrung, constrained. Compromised, suboptimal outputs. Overall risk not reduced, just spread around, possibly even increased. False sense of security in numbers: Undue risk-taking may be greater.
Open or Network Alliances	A flourishing network, web, or ecosystem of co-innovators. Encourage developers and users. Push technology adoption, create installed base. Positive feedback—alliance success breeds greater success. Create a rising tide for all within your network, web, or ecosystem. Set standards, "the" standard. Build a defensible network.	Great for setting standards, creating "public goods," pushing adoption. Not great for profits: interoperable standards, "public goods" at odds with any one firm's competitive advantage. A rising tide advantages no firm and benefits flow to other stakeholders (e.g., customers, suppliers). In contrast, a proprietary-dominated network might be highly profitable, but that's not an alliance—it's dominance by a core technology and/or market leader, with others playing follow-the-leader.
Integral Strategic Alliances	Similar to joint venture. . . . Bring together complementary resources and capabilities. Synergies, joint learning. Increase speed, strength, heft of innovation. Share innovation costs. Share innovation risks. Reduce risks and potential losses . . . But integrally monitored and managed by the parent firms.	Not completely free from the problems of JVs and consortia, but simpler and more focused overall. Fewer partners and no wholly independent (joint venture) entity means fewer inherent tensions and conflicts. Active, direct monitoring and management by the parents means problems can be realized earlier, addressed faster, and more easily. Inherently tend to be more integrated with, and supportive of, each firm's core innovation agendas and needs.

Toward More Focused Innovation Alliances

Despite all the potential pitfalls of innovation collaboration, it *can* be enormously productive and profitable even for *core* innovation tasks. But such alliances most often are best kept tightly integrated, monitored, and controlled, not set loose with a life and a will of their own. This is our conclusion after thoroughly reviewing more than 100 different forms and types of innovation alliances in a wide variety of industries. The one form of alliance we have not yet discussed—strategic alliances directly between partners, typically focused on specific research, development, and commercialization objectives—is frequently the most efficient and effective means of innovation collaboration. By this, we mean clearly targeted alliances that are created, monitored, and managed directly between the parent partners. Often there is no independent entity with its own charter and agenda or, if so, it might be a function of legal requirements and other formalities, more than by strategic need or organizational design.

Such alliances are increasingly common in technology-intensive sectors, but they run the gamut. Starbucks and PepsiCo were successful with their North American Coffee Partnership (NACP), for example, starting in 1995. NACP was formed to produce and sell ready-to-drink, bottled coffee products (for example, shelf-stable Starbucks Frappuccino) through a variety of retail outlets. It was a modest commercialization joint venture in many senses. But it succeeded notably where others had failed, including giants Kraft and Nestle. Some of the reasons for its success were basic. The joint venture brought together the complementary assets of Starbucks, the most recognized name in premium coffee beverages, with Pepsi and its powerful distribution network, finely-tuned to push bottled beverages through innumerable and diverse retail channels.

The reasons for NACP's success also were as much due to the underlying logic and structure of the alliance itself. The parent companies, Starbucks and Pepsi, were not competitors in any significantly direct sense. The joint venture had very clear and simple and focused objectives—producing and pushing ready-to-drink, bottled coffee products through retail channels such as grocery and convenience stores. Another key success factor was that, whatever the novelty of the product, the joint venture did not involve a critical product for either partner. Starbucks remained centered around delivering "the coffee experience," crafting and serving espresso drinks to customers in its own barista-staffed cafés. For Pepsi, ready-to-drink coffee was not a "killer category" like its other core beverage offerings (e.g., carbonated soft drinks). Even this successful example therefore shows how joint venturing often is relatively more fitting for the tasks of complementary, but relatively non-core, innovation.

Higher Stakes, More Potential Problems

Disney's lucrative partnership with Pixar shows that alliances for the purpose of core innovation tend to be more problematic. The stakes simply are higher. Animated films, from *Snow White* to *The Lion King,* were the heart and history of Disney's success. Following Disney's *The Lion King* blockbuster in 1994, it became clear that animation was evolving from the old hand-drawn labor of love into a new type of digital artistry. Disney had little competence in such hi-tech wizardry. Pixar, the computer animation company led by Apple co-founder Steve Jobs, became Disney's entry into the digital age. Pixar provided the hi-tech expertise to create the films, while Disney co-financed and distributed them.

Disney-Pixar seemed like a very powerful and complementary pairing. Indeed, it was. Beginning with *Toy Story* in 1995, the Disney-Pixar partnership produced a series of hugely successful films (including *A Bug's Life* and *Monsters, Inc.*). Indeed, Disney-Pixar's

2003 release *Finding Nemo* was the highest grossing animated film ever. By 2004, the partnership's films had generated more than $2.5 billion in box-office sales alone—not to mention videos, merchandise, and everything else.

But success caused friction. With the ten-year relationship up for renegotiation, the partners clashed over management, artistic control, and profits. Pixar demanded more of all three. Disney balked, and Pixar walked. Disney faced losing a future stream of digital blockbusters, even as its own internally produced animated films had increasingly disappointed fans and investors alike (for example, the massive flop *Treasure Planet* in late 2002).

Had Disney's success with Pixar lulled it into complacence? Now, Pixar was poised to be a powerful competitor, even as Disney's own digital capabilities remained limited. Meanwhile, Disney had slashed its animation division and, even according to namesake nephew Roy Disney, lost much of its creative edge. Disney's traditional animation core looked weak, and its digital future uncertain. Refurbishing the Disney legacy for the digital age would take significant cash and toil.

Pursuing Direct, Active, Engaged Partnerships

Despite such common tensions, close and focused collaboration nonetheless can make compelling sense for the tasks of core innovation. The biotechnology and pharmaceutical industries provide key examples. The usual scenario, of course, is that a small startup links its scientific discovery and promising new compounds with the cash and muscle of a big pharmaceutical company. The startups have the basic ideas and the big partners have the resources and capabilities needed to push investigational new drugs all the way through final clinical trials and out into the marketplace. A drug-licensing deal is often the result. As with other such integral alliances, there often is no formal third-party entity to complicate matters (such as a joint venture or consortium itself). Instead, the partnership directly brings together complementary assets and roles that are closely monitored and actively managed by both partners. The joint venture does not have a life and mind of its own. These types of alliances are not without their own difficulties. But with a relatively simplified structure and organization, and active ongoing management, problems can be more readily recognized and more quickly resolved.

The partnership of Trimeris, a small biotechnology company, and Roche, the large European-based pharmaceutical company, provides a good example of such integral innovation collaboration. In 1999, Trimeris and Roche agreed to cooperate to bring to market a new class of therapies for drug-resistant HIV strains. Unlike existing anti-HIV drugs, Trimeris's fusion inhibitors did not aim at stopping HIV from replicating after it invaded a cell. Instead, the new compounds promised to stop the virus from entering the cell in the first place. Trimeris had the basic science, had successfully gone public, and had funded and completed the basic development and initial phases of testing. At this stage, many technology companies start thinking about a future of licensing deals.

The Trimeris-Roche discussions begged for more than just another typical licensing agreement. Beyond the need to complete clinical trials and market the drugs, Trimeris's compounds presented a host of more exceptional challenges. Traditional chemistry produces small molecule drugs that are relatively easy to produce once formulated. Trimeris's discoveries were not typical, chemical-based, small-molecule pharmaceuticals. They were long and complex peptides, chains of amino acids similar to (but not quite) proteins. For patients, in practical terms, this also meant that the drugs would need to be injected. Trimeris's compounds would be much more difficult and costly to produce and deliver than the usual pill. Trimeris needed a substantial partner who could help further fund and develop relatively novel, complicated, and expensive manufacturing and delivery processes. As Roche noted, Fuzeon (as the lead compound would be named) was "one of the most complex and challenging molecules ever chemically manufactured on a large scale by the pharmaceutical industry."

Trimeris and Roche initially agreed to share equally both the development expenses and profits in the U.S. and Canada. Roche would commercialize and market the drugs elsewhere, paying royalties to Trimeris. The anti-HIV compounds soon received "fast track" status from the U.S. FDA. By 2000, Fuzeon entered Phase III clinical trials and Trimeris' continued to transfer its complex peptide-manufacturing knowledge to Roche's production facilities in Colorado.

In 2001, the partnership was expanded as the venture progressed. Under the terms of a new three-year agreement, renewable thereafter on an annual basis, Trimeris and Roche would equally fund worldwide research, development, and commercialization, as well as equally share the profits from worldwide sales, of any new HIV fusion inhibitor peptides. By 2003, Fuzeon received approval from the FDA and, especially because of the unfortunate rise of drug-resistant HIV, Roche literally could not produce enough of it to meet demand.

Avoiding Joint Problems

Trimeris and Roche's successful partnership is an example of how innovation alliances can be essential, fruitful, and profitable—even, in some cases, to tackle the tasks of core innovation. But if it's really a core issue, such collaboration must be closely monitored by and tightly integrated with its parents. Elan Pharmaceuticals's near collapse in 2002 provides a useful and interesting contrast. The Ireland-based drug company had numerous promising new compounds under development for a wide variety of conditions. However,

Elan chose to push the development of each drug as part of a complex web of several dozen independently incorporated joint ventures. In return, Elan got to dump expensive drug development costs onto these joint ventures, even while registering revenues by selling technology licenses to them. This R&D joint venture structure made Elan's own corporate performance appear much richer and healthier.

In late 2001, however, heightened scrutiny over Elan's innumerable joint ventures raised many concerns. Fancy financial accounting gimmicks suddenly were out of style. Few could make sense of the company's workings or its true worth. Elan's market value quickly plunged from $20 billion to less than $1 billion, accompanied by a series of lawsuits, investigations, and management turmoil. Elan subsequently divested many, and reconsolidated the rest, of its previously "independently" joint-ventured drugs. It did not eliminate all its drug development partnerships by any means; instead, it just brought the ones it retained back into account and back under control.

After a couple years of quiet retrenching, Elan bounced back. In early 2004, just one of its targeted development alliances with Biogen had notable success when its multiple sclerosis drug Antegren was approved by the U.S. FDA. Elan's market capitalization quickly increased ten-fold.

Elan's saga illustrates a recurring theme and one of our own main points. The *how* of innovation matters as much as the *what*. Elan had numerous compounds under development, each with fantastic promise. There was no shortage of real science or real promise. Its too-novel, off-the-books joint venture approach to developing these drugs, however, brought it great troubles. As with all the other innovation options we discuss, alliances must be formed for the right reasons, and in the right way, to maximize their chances of success. If they're crucial to a firm's core innovation needs and challenges, they probably need to be tightly managed as such—not as loosely structured and lightly managed organizations of their own accord.

5

R&D BY M&A
Innovation by Acquisition

"Every startup in the world is our R&D lab. If we can't build it, we'll just buy it."

—Telecom Executive in 2000

One way to avoid the potential problems of venturing, licensing, or partnering was simply to *acquire* innovation—literally. Don't venture to do it yourself and don't mess with the complexities of licensing or the compromises of partnering. Instead, just buy it outright. As companies struggled to hurdle radical technology shifts and juggle greater technological complexity, the idea of acquiring more and more innovation at earlier and earlier stages—even at previously unheard of prices—gained unprecedented appeal. From optics to genomics, so began the great R&D M&A boom.

Never had M&A markets seen anything like the innovation-by-acquisition binge that climaxed in 2000. The inflated stock of acquirers readily financed even richer acquisition purchase prices. At its peak, bankers put together hundreds of technology deals per quarter. Most of these deals remained more traditional buyouts of high-tech companies with real products, revenues, and profits. Increasingly, however, competitors began to bid up and buy more and earlier stage R&D in process. The acquired firms often had little other than unproven technologies or untested prototypes. Sometimes, it was technical talent alone that motivated quick and rich deals.

As with other innovation fads and fashions, however, things turned down as hard and fast as they had shot up. Much heralded, blockbuster innovation deals abruptly turned into spoiled projects and massive, mind-numbing write-downs. Some estimates placed the excess of the entire overall M&A wave at more than $1 trillion. Technology companies topped the roster of record-breaking M&A losses: JDS Uniphase, Nortel, Lucent, and others.

The aftermath of the innovation-by-acquisition binge should not have been completely surprising. Over the years, studies have shown that anywhere from half to two-thirds of M&A deals disappoint and destroy value for their acquirers. Most M&As fail either because the logic for the deal was flawed to begin with, because the price paid was simply too high, or because post-deal integration was bungled. This time around, it would be different, however. It was an entirely new model. Innovation by acquisition had been worked out to a science.

Unfortunately, R&D M&A deals presented their own special problems. The urgency of the go-go technology-driven deals meant rushed bids, higher prices, and limited due diligence. Some buyers didn't fully understand the newfangled intangibles for which they were paying richly. The assets being acquired were not solid businesses with real cash flows. Instead, they were ever-more raw and unproven, and often ephemeral, ideas and technologies. Retaining the acquired firm's top talent therefore was even more critical to making the deals work. But the best and most valuable employees sometimes just walked out the door before the ink on the deal had dried.

Why the Acquisition Boom?

The innovation-by-acquisition boom brought together the cutting edge of high technology and high finance in an especially frothy combination. It was both a cause and an effect of soaring financial markets and of a blossoming multitude of new technologies and new startup companies. The next largest historical wave of M&A in the 1980s had been primarily driven by consolidation and restructuring concerns, usually of mature companies in established or even declining industries. By the mid 1990s, a dramatic change in M&A attitudes got underway: "Companies are being acquired for quick access to scarce talent . . . Some of these buyers couldn't care less about product lines, plants, equipment, or real estate."[1] Many of the targets were VC-funded startups heavy in ideas and talent, but poor in real assets or cash flow. Seeing quick-and-rich exit strategies, they were more than happy to oblige their eager buyers.

For big companies trying to compete with increasingly tech-savvy upstarts, the motto became "If you can't beat 'em, buy 'em." Cisco Systems, among others, claimed that all Silicon Valley was its R&D lab. If you can't (or simply didn't) do the R&D yourself, just purchase it wholesale. The classic "make-or-buy" decision no longer applied just to low value-added nuts and bolts, but to the core of R&D itself. According to the Securities Data Corporation, biotechnology, electronics, IT services, networking, semiconductors, software, and telecommunications became among the most active M&A sectors by the late 1990s. The currency also had changed. The overwhelming majority of these deals were paid for with stock. High equity valuations across the board made even the most high-priced purchases seem relatively painless.

Innovation by Acquisition

The idea of innovation by acquisition was not entirely novel. At least when established industry leaders couldn't outright crush, intimidate, or out-invent them, young and innovative startups had long been favored acquisition targets. Moreover, despite all the outsized attention paid to glitzy public offerings, such as Netscape's huge 1995 IPO, acquisition always had been the predominant exit or liquidity strategy for most startups. Before, during, and after the technology bubble, the vast majority of innovative entrepreneurial firms never came anywhere near a public offering, but rather were acquired.

One 1999 analysis by Broadview International, for example, found that almost 1,900 privately held technology firms had been acquired in the previous year, while only 147 had gone public. This was overwhelmingly true even for VC-backed technology firms. Similarly, data from Venture Economics showed that the total number of venture-backed IPOs plummeted to 35 in 2001 and then only 22 in 2002. But the number of venture-backed firms acquired totaled 336 in 2001 and remained stable through 2002. Valuations were down by 75 percent or more, but a steady and quiet stream of deals continued. At least now the prices were more reasonable.

The New Wave of R&D M&A

What was different about the new New Economy innovation-by-acquisition craze was the number and speed of deals and, especially, the astronomical valuations paid for companies acquired at earlier and earlier stages of development. By contrast, even the most colossal New Economy–Old Economy merger, the ill-fated AOL–Time Warner deal, was more of a traditional M&A transaction than an

R&D-driven marriage. AOL was not some small, unknown startup with a newfangled technology. It was the dominant Internet service provider, with tens of millions of customers and a well-established brand name. As superlative and disappointing as the $100 billion plus AOL deal was, it did not necessarily represent radically new M&A thinking, just the incredibly inflated values and expectations of the time.

In contrast, the new wave of innovation acquisitions was distinguished by acquirers who were buying companies primarily or solely for their R&D-in-process or technical talent. Tallies of revenues, profits, and cash flow were of little use in evaluating such deals because the target firms simply had none. New metrics were dreamed up. P/E no longer stood for price-to-earnings ratio. For some R&D M&A deals, P/E instead was shorthand for price-per-engineer. The price could be steep. Deals for companies with little or no sales or tangible assets, much less profits, went as high as $20–25 million or more per engineer, programmer, or scientist.[2] Untested technologies, unproven products, and pure R&D talent itself became more of a primary, if not sole, acquisition objective.

The quantity and value of technology deals soared. According to Securities Data Corporation, the number of software acquisitions grew from fewer than 100 deals in 1985 to more than 1,100 deals by 1998. The growth was not simply a function of the general boom in M&A activity during the same period, either. Software M&A rose dramatically as a proportion of total deals, from approximately 3 percent in 1985 to more than 14 percent by 1998. Then, the innovation-by-acquisition spree really got started.

Cisco the Serial Acquirer

No company exemplified the innovation-by-acquisition trend more than Cisco Systems. During the 1990s, Cisco grew phenomenally. By the end of the decade, for a very brief period, Cisco peaked as the most valuable company in the world in terms of market capitalization, besting even Microsoft, at more than half a trillion dollars. The Cisco growth story was fueled by an accelerating series of acquisitions, both big and small.

Cisco's roster of deals began in 1993 with its $90 million purchase of Crescendo Communications. Within just a few years, the technologies and products at the heart of the Crescendo acquisition would become Cisco's largest single business. Throughout the 1990s, Cisco acquired dozens more young companies, for everything from software to hardware, to fill out its technology and product portfolio:

> No company typifies the new world of M&A better than Cisco Systems. To understand how it has built its empire, it is necessary to forget all that one knows about corporate raiders and their swashbuckling tactics. Disregard the stereotypes of ruthless capitalist villains aiming to gobble up corporate America's finest . . . Think of Cisco as an acquisition engine, as cleverly designed and highly tuned as the giant routers it builds to handle vast surges of Internet traffic. Like those routers, the acquisition engine runs on Internet time. In the past 6 years, Cisco has spent $18.8 billion on 42 acquisitions. It prowls Silicon Valley—and the world—snapping up companies to expand existing product lines or support entirely new initiatives.[3]

Cisco set the trend and the pace. Its ever-upward stock seemed to be a limitless currency with which to do deals, creating a virtuous cycle.

Over time, Cisco's own acquisition strategy evolved. The networking leader began to acquire younger new startups at earlier and earlier stages of development. By the end of the 1990s, it had switched from acquiring up-and-coming companies with fantastic new products and booming sales to acquiring more and more R&D in process. By 1999 and into 2000, the process shifted into overdrive. Cisco was acquiring a new company every few weeks. Purchase prices soared. An entire gaggle of high-tech startups came into being with the specific hope and plan to be a quick and rich Cisco deal.

After just seven years, by the peak of the market bubble in March 2000, Cisco had acquired 52 companies. The tab totaled more than $20 billion, but it seemed to be more than worth the price. Cisco undisputedly was the world leader in the lucrative, can't-build-it-fast-enough hardware that powered the Internet. Cisco became the model to emulate. Many subsequently did try to imitate Cisco and even exceed its acquisitive zeal.

Not that Cisco was easy to top. Cerent was the deal that certified the beginning of a new era. Cerent was a hot new optical Internet router maker preparing to go public in mid 1999. Cisco was strong in electronics, but relatively weak in optical technology. The entire telecom and Internet world seemed destined to go optical, however, and optical was Cerent's strength. Cisco already owned 8 percent of the startup from an earlier, exploratory investment. In August 1999, Cisco pre-empted Cerent's IPO and offered a jaw-dropping $7 billion in stock to buy the rest of the company outright.

The rich price was literally unprecedented. Cisco's previously highest-priced deal, $4 billion for StrataCom in 1996, had bought it a profitable company of 1,000 employees with more than $300 million in revenues. In contrast, Cerent had fewer than 300 employees, just $10 million in revenues, and a loss of $29 million for 1999 to date. All the value was in Cerent's potential; there was little else by which to value it. Using one of the novel M&A metrics of the time, some noted that the deal cost Cisco almost $25 million per employee. Cerent's owners certainly were happy. Only a month earlier, the company had announced its plans for a public offering to raise just $100 million.

Changing R&D Paradigms

The new innovation-by-acquisition approach contrasted significantly with the old R&D design. This contrast could be seen clearly by comparing Cisco's evolution with that of Lucent Technologies. Over the decades, Lucent had nurtured its Bell Labs into a Nobel Prize-winning nurturer of all kinds of scientific and technical talent. Through its lucrative telephone monopoly, AT&T (Lucent's parent until 1996) steadily and handsomely funded Bell Labs.

By the time of Lucent's spin off, however, the telecom market-place had already begun to be much more fiercely competitive and much more fast-moving and complex on the operating and technical side. The old scholarly, gentlemanly approach to R&D increasingly seemed to be a bygone luxury. New up-and-coming engineers dreamed less of building a career at Bell Labs and more of joining a hot new technology startup. Making the situation even more complex, traditional telecom and the Internet began to blur. The old, safe and steady business of selling gear to established long-distance providers and local telephone monopolies started to turn into a scramble to provide better and faster technologies to both new and old telecom and networking companies alike.

But Lucent initially resisted joining in the innovation-by-acquisition frenzy. The company had a long and distinguished history of world-class internal R&D excellence and a strongly inward-focused engineering culture. In practical terms, Lucent's reluctance to deal also stemmed from pooling-of-interest restrictions related to its spinoff from AT&T. Any big acquisition purchases would take a big bite directly out of Lucent's financials. These accounting constraints expired late in 1998, however, letting Lucent more freely consider its options.

Meanwhile, the pressure on Lucent had grown. Telecom giant Alcatel had acquired networker DSC Communications in mid 1998 for $4.4 billion. In a similar move, Northern Telecom acquired Bay Networks for more than $9 billion, even changing its name to Nortel Networks in the process. Newly freed from its accounting chains, Lucent finally signaled that it would not be left behind the dawning digital age. The stakes were high. In December 1998, Lucent acquired networker Ascend Communications for more than $20 billion. The big deals seemed strategically sound, even if they were increasingly somewhat pricey. They brought not only new R&D and technology to their acquirers, but also substantial revenues and customers from already well-established networking industry leaders. They were just warm-ups for the deal sprint about to begin.

Cisco's Cerent acquisition in August 1999 was the starting gun. Technological and competitive urgency grew, and the relative pace and size of deals soared. The science of R&D and the art of the deal, the mysterious alchemy of technology and finance, became increasingly intertwined. It was not always clear which drove which.

Network equipment startup Siara Systems had yet to test a product in November 1999, but Redback Networks offered $4.7 billion for it nonetheless.[4] Privately held optical transmission startup Qtera did not yet have a product on the market; Nortel paid $3.25 billion for it in December 1999. Nortel added to its string of deals in March 2000 with its acquisition of Xros, a photonics switching company also with no revenue or product shipped, also for $3.25 billion. Responding in kind, Lucent acquired fiber equipment maker Chromatis in May 2000. Chromatis was just two years old and had not yet shipped a single product. Lucent offered $4.75 billion. Quickly, Cisco and the old-line telecom manufacturers started to look much more alike, in more ways than one.

In a world of supposedly rational and efficient markets, executives, analysts, and academics alike scrambled for new justifications for such stratospheric deal valuations. The old rules no longer applied. Valuation seemed to become storytelling and cheerleading as much as science. The only justification needed for some high deal prices was a "comp" (comparable), meaning an astronomical price became justified simply because someone else, for whatever reason, might be willing to pay as much or more. Was it all really worth it?

Need for Speed, Technology, and Talent

The need for speed was probably the most often-cited deal driver and a key justification for high prices. In the fast-moving, hypercompetitive New Economy, the dominant view was that, in so many new and rapidly transforming industries, the window of opportunity wouldn't remain open for long. It wasn't just for telecom and the Internet. It was also in biotech, semiconductors, and any number of other sectors. Tomorrow wasn't good enough. Companies felt the compelling need for the latest-and-greatest technology *today*.

Internally, acquirers couldn't do R&D fast enough, no matter how much money they were willing and able to throw at a problem. Even if Cisco Systems were willing and able to spend $7 billion R&D to try to develop its own optical routers, for example, the feeling (both inside and outside the company) was that it would simply take too long. It was faster to buy R&D in process from Cerent than to try to assemble and build a technical team from scratch. First to product and market, if not the only thing, was usually at least a compelling goal. Certainly, at least being fast to market, even if not first, was essential. The perceived need for R&D speed fit perfectly with the larger, pervasive creed of first-mover advantage.

If companies didn't have enough urgency themselves, they were pushed to get technologically acquisitive by analysts and investors. The rewards and punishments dealt by the financial markets were contrary to their reactions in more traditional M&A deals. The stocks of companies doing R&D acquisition deals, even at exorbitant prices, got pushed higher. Stocks of companies that hesitated or refused stalled or were even punished. It became easy to make the self-justifying argument that the absence of a blockbuster R&D deal could easily lop billions or more off a company's market capitalization. Analysts and investors would turn their backs and bail on such technological laggards—the ones that "just didn't get it."

Rich deal prices also seemed unavoidable in a context of grossly overvalued (technology) stocks in general. It was better to buy a privately held startup quickly and now, even for billions, than to potentially face a bidding war later and pay billions more, or to pay even greater sums after a company went public. This calculus was not pure speculation. Networking, optical, and other technology companies that did go public during this era quickly reached valuations in the billions (for example, JDS Uniphase and Juniper Networks).

Dozens of innovation-by-acquisition deals were done quickly and richly specifically to preempt the need for even richer post-IPO transactions. The need for speed rapidly became a self-fulfilling prophecy. Leading companies quickly snapped up any and all potential technology targets. If you didn't act fast, there might not be anything left. This pressure was most extreme in telecom and networking, but it quickly grew to encompass almost any sector in which radical new technologies and unique technical talents were at a premium: software and semiconductors, pharmaceuticals and biotechnology and bioinformatics, and so on.

Radical Technologies and Unique Talents

What powered many of the highest-value, highest-profile deals was the New Economy–Old Economy divide. Beginning in the mid 1990s, for example, Monsanto and DuPont bid against each other and spent billions to acquire a series of agricultural biotechnology concerns at ever-higher prices. Both chemical giants attempted to leap from commodity chemicals into a brave new world of more lucrative, genetically engineered bioscience. Likewise, telecom manufacturers tried to conquer the new world of networking, and electronics firms tried to make the leap to new optical technologies. They faced fundamentally altered technical challenges and befuddling new business models. Meanwhile, traditional, trial-and-error, chemical-focused pharmaceutical firms confronted an entirely new array of high-throughput screening, targeted genomics, and biotechnology-generated proteins. Their decades of accumulated drug-discovery knowledge suddenly seemed much less relevant, even antiquated. In contrast, their acquisition targets appeared to have mastered these radical new technologies. They also had the world-class, one-of-a-kind brainpower and technical wizardry needed to continue to further develop and deploy them.

Sometimes, talent alone was a critical objective:

> [E]ngineers and scientists are still in high demand, so much so that semiconductor and optical networking outfits are doing more of what bankers call HR deals (HR for Human Resources). In these acquisitions the employees are seen as more valuable than the company's product.[5]

The battle for technical talent even spawned a new valuation calculus:

> [I]t's human capital companies are after. A potential target's value is determined by the number of engineers it employs and their skill set.[6]

Talent markets grew tight. Salaries, stock options, and benefits soared. Deals at $2 million per employee that had raised eyebrows in 1997 soon were eclipsed by $20 million per employee deals just two or three years later. The intensifying competition for talent meant that retaining the services of increasingly scarce knowledge workers—innovators such as top programmers, engineers, and scientists, as well as creative types—required buying entire companies. It was not enough to pick up a few engineers here and there. M&A was the only way to get enough good talent quickly.

Once again, Cisco helped set the tone. Cisco's attention to the details of implementation, especially talent retention, was thought to be key to its many acquisition successes. It wasn't always a completely smooth process, but Cisco tried to learn from its early acquisition stumbles. Subsequently, the company had instituted a more detailed plan and process for integration.

CEO John Chambers noted that most of what Cisco was doing was acquiring people. It placed great emphasis on keeping acquired employees happy to retain their skills long after the acquisition deal was done. The company was frequently featured as unusually successful at retaining key acquired employees—at least more so than most acquirers. Cisco gave them generous option grants, communicated openly and frequently during the acquisition process to reduce uncertainty, and rapidly integrated them into important roles within the overall Cisco team and culture. Most firms did not seem to pay nearly as much attention to these "softer" issues and did not address them with such forethought. When paying millions of dollars per employee in an ongoing war for talent, acquiring and retaining key employees was not a "soft" or trivial issue.[7] It was central to the task of innovation.

The Deal-Making Denouement

Overall M&A activity reached historic heights in 1999 and 2000, with over $3 trillion in deals globally each year. Just a year later, the total value of M&A deals dropped to about a third of those levels; the number of deals dropped less, but still dramatically. Stock had been the boom-time currency of choice. Now, cash was king again as the majority of sellers demanded hard currency. As the general

M&A boom went bust, so did innovation by acquisition. Frenetic, high-priced R&D M&A deals abruptly disappeared.

Again, except this time on the downside, Cisco set the pace. In 1999, Cisco bought 30 companies. By 2000, the number dropped to 11. For all 2001, Cisco acquired just two companies: Allegro Technologies and AuroraNetics. Cisco slowed its gusher M&A pipeline to a trickle. Amid the crumbling of the telecom sector and the sputtering of the networking business, Cisco retrenched, laid off, and downsized. The company decided to focus more on tapping the internal brainpower and invention of its own thousands of engineers and to rely less on acquisitions. It was a sea-change in strategy, an apparently radical break from its own innovation-by-acquisition legacy.[8] Even Mike Volpi, the celebrated strategist and deal maker for most of Cisco's serial acquisitions, transitioned to a different, daily, operating role as senior vice president of Cisco's routing technology group.

The frenzied deal-making days were clearly over. In retrospect, there was consensus both within and outside the company that Cisco's later acquisitions especially had not been nearly as successful as they had initially appeared. The technology and products were more problematic, the integration less smooth, and the added growth much less than hoped and planned. As it surfed the massive wave of Internet growth, most anything fast-growing Cisco did would have seemed brilliant. Now, for both itself and other would-be imitators, Cisco's innovation-by-acquisition success during the 1990s seemed much more an exceptional historical episode rather than a durable new model for innovation. Moreover, in practical terms, Cisco's stock no longer was the "better than gold" currency that it had been.

The giddy deal-making days ended. Proponents of any new Cisco acquisitions would be held responsible to commit to their financial results, not just hype a great new technology. Even Cisco's March 2003 acquisition of Linksys for $500 million, its most expensive purchase since 2000, was a return to a more grounded type of M&A deal. Linksys was already the leader in home wireless-networking gear; it was not a quick speculative bet on unproven technology or raw talent. Linksys was an established company with proven products and real revenue. With sales of $430 million in 2002, Linksys commanded a very modest price of just a little more than one times revenue.

Hangover from an R&D M&A Binge

The aftermath of the R&D M&A boom and bust is surprisingly difficult to assess clearly and objectively. Even in hindsight, it's difficult to get meaningful agreement among entrepreneurs, executives, analysts, or academics on which deals made sense and which did not, how much the rich prices were justified and necessary, or whether they simply represented the height of the irrational exuberance of the times. Even well after the fact, great disagreement exists about the logic and performance of many of the priciest, high-profile deals. In the telecom and networking sectors, for example, there is no control group with which to compare non-acquirers and aggressive acquirers; almost all the leading firms actively participated in the innovation-by-acquisition binge and at extremely high prices.

It's also not easy to pick an agreeable metric. Does the fact that the stock of a Cisco, Lucent, Nortel, or JDS Uniphase was itself fantastically overvalued excuse the fact that these companies' acquisition deals were even more overpriced? Does the fact that some of these acquisitions did not pan out and were simply shuttered reflect a massively failed innovation strategy or instead just reflect the inherently uncertain and risky nature of R&D and innovation in general?

Goodwill Gone Bad

One way to assess the aftermath, of course, is to examine the numbers. Accounting complexities and other convenient justifications aside, goodwill write downs in the aftermath of M&A deals more often than not are an implicit admission that a buyer simply paid too much for acquired assets. What remains of the acquired firm is worth less than the purchase price.[9] In this regard at least, the bottom line (literally) was that record-setting innovation-driven M&A deals quickly were transformed into record-setting write downs and losses.

In 2001, for example, fiber-optic components maker JDS Uniphase took more than $50 billion in goodwill write downs, most of which reflected the devaluation of its high-priced acquisitions. The total was the largest asset impairment charge in U.S. corporate history. Dramatic reductions in the value of three 2000 acquisitions in particular—its $41 billion purchase of SDL, its $18 billion transaction for E-Tek Dynamics, and its $2.8 billion deal for Optical Coating Laboratory—accounted for most of the losses. Obviously, some observers thought the losses indicated that JDS Uniphase's acquisition strategy had seriously stumbled. Others disagreed, including management:

> From [JDS CFO] Muller's perspective, however, the acquisitions JDS made during the capital spending Brigadoon firmed its position as a leading fiber optic component maker, and the mountain of goodwill the company accrued in doing so was justifiable. The employee talent and technologies JDS garnered were invaluable, and if Muller knew then what he knows now, he wouldn't change a thing.[10]

Some outsiders agreed. The $50 billion write down and massive losses were meaningless. They were purely cosmetic, even if they were nominally as large as the entire GDP of New Zealand. It didn't really matter; it was not real money. It was simply an accounting charge, a formality to comply with new bookkeeping rules, with no real cash flow implications. Ignore it.

Cash or Stock: Play Money?

This perspective raises some curious questions. How can a $50 billion loss *not* be a reflection of a problem, in some way, at some point? If accounting-based performance measures are meaningless, by which metrics *should* performance be measured? Did having paid in (especially inflated) stock, rather than cash, make even overpriced acquisitions not really a problem? After all, no "real" money was exchanged or lost.

The problem with this logic is that stock is not play money. It has real value—including real cash value—that begs to be taken more seriously. Ultimately, $1 of stock equals $1 of value, regardless of accounting complexities and other justifications. Opportunity cost considerations make the assessment even more complex. What else could a company have bought? Or could acquirers simply have waited and then acquired the same companies for a fraction of their original asking price, after valuations had plummeted? Of course, by then the buyers' own stocks had plummeted as well, dropping their shares 90 percent or more in some cases. Cash prices might have dropped precipitously, but the number of shares required to purchase the same company might have been even greater than before. With such strange deal-making math, it's a bit easier to explain, if not excuse, at least some key aspects of the stock-fueled M&A mania.

Not all these acquisitions were paid for in inflated stock, however. Cash deals make the hit from disappointing acquisitions seem more real, even if theoretically no difference between stock and cash exists. Corning, for example, acquired Pirelli's optical components business in December 2000, paying $3.6 billion in cash. In early 2001, however, Corning took more than $3 billion in charges to reflect a severe decline in the acquired assets' value. In just months, most of the deal's cash purchase price had evaporated. Corning claimed that this did not mean they had overpaid for the acquisition, but rather simply reflected the fact that telecom markets had turned down suddenly and dramatically. Whatever the explanation, the loss was just as big.

In the aftermath of the innovation-by-acquisition deflation, Cisco Systems CEO John Chambers expressed the now more sober deal-making calculus. Whether stock or cash, he stressed, it was ultimately the same deal. Both came out of shareholders' pockets, either from the firm's cash reserves or as diluted shares. Deal-making shares probably would be paid off in cash eventually anyway, with share buybacks necessary to reduce shareholder dilution. Times and attitudes clearly had changed; the pendulum had swung back toward more grounded M&A attitudes. The need for speed, technology, and talent no longer justified acquiring innovation at any cost.

Addicted to Speed

Apart from the problem of greatly inflated prices, was the underlying logic of innovation by acquisition (especially R&D by M&A) still sound? The need for speed, technology, and talent seemed a compelling trio of innovation motives and objectives. Did the R&D M&A boom still more fundamentally represent a significant and sustained shift toward a new paradigm for innovation, as so many of its proponents had proclaimed? Or was it just another temporary craze, like much of the rest of the technology and market mania of the time? Perhaps it was a bit of both.

For example, was the "need for speed" a sound logic for such quick-and-rich deals in the first place? Certainly in hindsight, the urgency seemed overdone. Even in many new and fast-growing industries, being the first or fastest tends to be an overrated success factor.[11] Moreover, the need for speed always comes with a price. Urgency costs in more ways than one. It means doing deals earlier, when technologies and markets are more embryonic and far from certain bets. Getting a deal done now also requires paying whatever

the seller or market demands; impatience inherently tends to raise the price.

Urgency also raises the likely cost of a deal because of the fact that there is simply less time for due diligence. During the height of the boom, multibillion-dollar deals were sometimes negotiated in just a few hours. Rushed due diligence raises the likelihood and magnitude of mispricing and other mistakes (such as buying a dud). In some cases, buyers didn't quite understand what they were buying at such rich prices; the acquired firm's radically new, different, and unfamiliar technology was what motivated most of the deals in the first place. With such dynamics in play, sellers can pitch a "lemon" and fetch a good price; sometimes, they did just that. All these issues characterized the R&D M&A binge and all played a role in the many subsequent disappointments.

If speed really were the prime success factor in most cases of innovation, it nonetheless might be worth the price and risk to engage in even expensive and uncertain R&D deals. But first-mover advantages often are more myth than reality.[12] Pioneers help pave the way for others, but the first companies to jump in a new technology or market more often fade or eventually fail. Meanwhile, strong followers gain and then maintain lasting technology and industry leadership. Slow and steady often does win the race. Even if being early is better—all things being equal—being the pioneer may not be the "crown jewel" that some companies seem willing to pay so much for. Execution speed is good, but more speed isn't necessarily always better.

Big Bucks, Little Results?

Even if being first or fastest wasn't essential, surely acquiring brand-new technologies and capabilities was worth doing many deals. In some cases, it was. Yet, with a number of R&D M&A, little was left to show for huge sums spent. In less than two years,

Nortel simply shut down the division it had formed with its $3.25 billion acquisition of Xros. Xros's technology for making an all-optical switch did not work as planned, was difficult to manufacture, and the optical market never materialized as anticipated. Similarly, less than a couple years after Nortel paid $3.25 billion for Qtera, the key technology and product that motivated the acquisition had simply faded away. Nortel's write downs for these and other deals totaled more than $12 billion in 2001. Nortel was far from alone. Lucent discontinued Chromatis's products in 2001 and took a nearly $4 billion write down as a result.

Even Cisco Systems, the master acquirer, was not immune to these risks. Cisco paid $500 million for Monterey Networks in August 1999. Monterey was developing optical networking routers, but did not yet have a fully developed product. Cisco hoped to bolster its own nascent optical networking business. After 18 months of technical problems, delays, and disappointing sales, however, in April 2001 Cisco announced that it would stop making the routers. The Monterey-based offerings disappeared. Neither the technology and product, nor the market itself, had worked out as planned. Unlike many of its peers, Cisco had long since chosen to expense, on an ongoing basis, most of the price of its acquisitions as in-process R&D. As a result, Cisco avoided a long list of its own goodwill write downs and losses.

These experiences highlight some of the key tradeoffs and dilemmas of innovation by acquisition, especially early-stage R&D M&A. Acquirers are making a bet. Much of the uncertainty and risk remains. Paying a rich, speculative price for a relatively early stage deal exacerbates these risks. In the aftermath of the R&D M&A wave, more sober valuations for these types of deals reflected a turn back toward a fundamental economic truth: Risk should be discounted, not inflated. Moreover, no matter how intrinsically valuable, even successful technology can never be truly profitable if its price is simply too high to begin with.

The Slippery Logic of Acquiring Talent

Acquiring top-notch, world-class technical and creative talent by itself sometimes seemed a compelling acquisition objective. But purchasing a firm does not equate to having retained the continued services (the loyalty, creativity, and productivity) of the acquired firm's top talent. Yet, this was a key presumption of many innovation-by-acquisition deals. It's entirely possible that much of the high-priced, high-potential talent will simply walk away soon after a deal is done.[13] With a change of control, turnover of key employees typically skyrockets. More unfortunately, top talent often leaves first; the best employees are obviously the ones with the greatest opportunities elsewhere. This is a common dilemma when companies aim to acquire top talent (such as entrepreneurs, engineers, scientists, programmers, artists and designers, project managers, and other key employees). A rich, high-premium deal price might end up buying little more than a hollow shell of a company with few people left to make things work.

Even Cisco, with a much better record of employee retention than most, had issues with turnover of acquired talent. Cisco's overall post-acquisition turnover rates might have been relatively low. But combing the record reveals some retention problems nonetheless:

> [Cisco CEO] Chambers often maintained that his acquisition strategy was aimed at acquiring brainpower more than products. But an analysis of the 18 acquisitions Cisco made in 1999 shows that Monterey was no fluke. Many of the most valuable employees, the highly driven founders and chief executives of these acquired companies, have since bolted, taking with them a good deal of the expertise and experience for which Cisco paid top dollar.

The two founders of StratumOne Communications Inc., a maker of optical semiconductors purchased for $435 million, left Cisco. The chief exec of GeoTel Communications Corp., a call-routing outfit acquired for $2 billion, walked out after nine months. So did the CEOs or founders of Sentient Networks, MaxComm Technologies, WebLine Communications, Tasmania Network Systems, Aironet Wireless Communications, V-Bits, and Worldwide Data Systems—all high-priced acquisitions in 1999. Some simply felt Cisco had become too big and too slow. "People who crave risk don't do so well at Cisco," says Narad Networks CEO Dev Gupta, who sold Dagaz and MaxComm Technologies Inc. to Cisco in 1997 and 1999, respectively. "Cisco focuses much more on immediate customer needs, less on high-wire technology development that customers may want two to three years out."

. . . After losing many of the leaders of these businesses, product delays and other mishaps were not uncommon. When Cisco closed down Monterey, for example, the company still hadn't put a product out for testing, which alone would take as long as a full year. "By the time the product was there to test, the market wasn't," says Joseph Bass, former CEO of Monterey.[14]

Another unfortunate M&A dysfunction was discord and discontent among existing Cisco employees. Some of the newly rich, newly acquired Cisco employees adopted a "new kids on the block" swagger, causing ill will among incumbent engineers who had toiled with Cisco for years, and whose own stock and options soon withered in value. Not only acquired talent left, but existing Cisco talent also departed.

Golden Handcuffs for Free Agents?

Most strategies to try to reduce or eliminate post-acquisition turnover of top talent have limited effectiveness at best. So-called "golden handcuffs"—the idea of bribing top talent in the acquired firm to stay after an M&A deal is done—are a nice metaphor. But they usually don't have the desired effect. In one study of a large number of hi-tech, talent-driven acquisitions in a wide variety of industries, the results revealed much: Across the board, golden handcuffs failed at a high rate. Neither restricted nor unrestricted stock options or grants, nor long-term contracts with cash and other bonuses, had significantly positive effects on retention of key employees.[15]

This was a recurring and significant problem for a large number of the more than 100 cases of innovation by acquisition we examined. One high-tech engineer/entrepreneur summed it up, "I had my desk packed before the ink [on the deal] was even dry." The deal itself had rewarded him quite well. Flush and comfortable, he already was on his way to thinking about the next startup opportunity, not about how to serve the new corporate master.

Talented Competition: Palm Versus Handspring

The saga of Palm versus Handspring illustrates well the tensions inherent in trying to acquire and retain top innovators. Here's the typical scenario: Acquired innovators uncomfortable with serving their new corporate masters yearn to break free. Instead of staying put, the top technical and entrepreneurial founders bolt, found a new firm, and sometimes even end up competing with their former masters. This was Handspring's story.

Donna Dubinsky and Jeff Hawkins founded Palm, the pioneering maker of personal digital assistants (PDAs). With their PDA product still in development and starved for cash, Palm needed assistance. U.S. Robotics, the leading modem supplier, came to the rescue and acquired Palm for $44 million. Apple's Newton might have come earlier (perhaps too early), but Palm became the first successful PDA. Unlike many earlier and clunkier concepts, Palm's PDA easily linked and synched with a standard PC. In 1997, more than one million Palm Pilots shipped. Palm was an unqualified success, literally the stuff of Silicon Valley legend.

Events took another turn, however, as 3Com acquired U.S. Robotics. Dubinsky and Hawkins pushed 3Com to spin out Palm and let it be free. They felt that the Palm concept and its potential would get shortchanged and suboptimized. Palm now was trapped within the confines of an even larger muddling-and-meddling corporate parent more concerned about cost-cutting and maintaining margins than growing an exciting new business.

3Com refused to let Palm go, so Dubinsky and Hawkins quit and hired a team of their own engineers. Venture capitalists (VCs) salivated and fought each other for the privilege of funding the duo's new company. Within a year, the Handspring Visor PDA was born. The Visor was a lower-cost "clone" of the Palm PDA, using the same operating system (licensed from Palm). Handspring innovated a step further by adding expansion-slot capabilities that allowed its PDA to become an MP3 player, phone, digital camera, and whatever else could be dreamed up and plugged in. It quickly captured almost one-third of the PDA market. Capping off this success, Handspring went public in mid 2000. Ironically, this was just three months after 3Com finally decided to spin out Palm after all, with its own IPO.

The Palm and Handspring rivalry grew. Competition turned to price wars, followed by big losses and layoffs for both players. Palm struggled, and Handspring itself was running short of cash. In 2003, completing the complicated saga, Palm agreed to acquire Handspring.[16] After battling each other for years, together again they finally would try to better compete against the new and rapidly proliferating mobile computing rivals (e.g., Microsoft-based and cell phone–based systems).

The Palm-Handspring saga is not an odd exception. Much top talent tends to leave in the wake of an acquisition; the best are most likely to leave, and likely to leave the fastest. Moreover, top teams tend to stick together—including when they leave. Golden handcuffs offer limited hope at best. Even when they reduce turnover, they still cannot buy top talent's loyalty, productivity, or creativity—the key intangibles that make the difference between success and failure. Overemphasis of non-compete agreements also misses the key point. Most acquired top talent doesn't necessarily leave to start a direct new competitor—although it does happen, and even despite non-compete agreements. Regardless, with significant post-deal turnover, top talent—and all their knowledge, skills, and relationships—might be lost either way.

Buying Innovation Still Can Be a Good Deal

As the previous examples highlight, innovation by acquisition has its own unique costs and risks. Despite these inherent dilemmas and formidable challenges, the M&A approach nonetheless represents a useful evolution (though not revolution) in the concept and practice of innovation strategy. Acquiring fast-growing technology companies with hot new products was not a new idea. What was relatively novel was the idea of acquiring more and earlier-stage R&D in process (R&D by M&A). In the aftermath of overzealous deal making, both early stage and later stage innovation deals assumed a more sober yet still important role in the innovation mix. But it also remains true that neither is a cheap and quick fix for core technology and talent needs.

When does innovation by acquisition make sense, and when is it worth the price? Many lessons can be learned by reflecting on the R&D M&A boom and bust. The excesses and errors of the period had less to do with a fatal flaw in the idea itself and instead had more to do with problems in its application and execution. Acquisitions were rushed because of a too-urgent "need for speed" to gain hot new technologies and capabilities. Hurried and limited due diligence in turn led to both too-high prices and high-priced duds and lemons. Overall frothiness in the financial markets did jack up the prices. But too-high deal prices also were a result of flawed risk/ reward discounting and fanciful valuation justifications. Ultimately, the considerable risks of paying richly for unproven new technologies, uncertain new markets, and fickle new talent were neither anticipated nor managed well. All these issues need to be (and fortunately can be) better tackled in contemplating, valuing, and executing innovation-driven acquisitions.

Bargain Shopping: Balancing Risk and Reward

These issues are especially critical in earlier stage deals (R&D M&A). The fundamental differences between early stage and later stage deals got blurred in the M&A frenzy. Early stage and later stage deals need to be evaluated, paid for, and planned for differently. Risks and rewards need to be balanced. Early stage R&D M&A deals can be sensible and fruitful bets to try to gain the potential of brand new talent, new patents, and new products and processes, for example. The farther they are from commercialization, however, the more the inherent uncertainty and risk should discount their value. R&D M&A deals also need to be adjusted accordingly to the degree that the target innovations depend on potentially fleeting intangibles, including talent itself.

The bottom line is that early stage R&D deals should be appropriately discounted, not inflated. Only then is risk properly compensated and, if the bet is successful, only then are the rich potential profits not already squandered at the moment of purchase. Moreover, bargains can be found for both early stage (R&D) and late stage innovations. Paradoxically, bargains abound most when, and largely because, buyers are scarce.

The irony is that many companies hesitated to do early stage R&D M&A deals just as prices for some valuable technology and talent was coming back into more reasonable (even bargain) price ranges. The result of this reluctance was foregone opportunities.

For those with the courage and cash, deals abounded. The valuations of VC-backed technology firms, in everything from biotechnology to semiconductors, tanked by 75 percent or more from 2000 to 2002. In some sectors, the discounts approached 90 percent. Moreover, with VCs stingy and with the IPO markets dried up, technology startups now were willing to settle for more agreeable purchase prices. The fundamental value of the startups' underlying technologies, ideas, and other assets had not changed in most cases. Only now they could be had for a fraction of their previous prices. According to Venture Economics, smart buyers kept the volume of VC-backed acquisition deals fairly constant from 2000 to 2002, even as average prices plummeted. Deals that formerly looked too big and risky suddenly looked like more reasonable bets.

Buyers snatched up high-quality biotech and genomics and software and semiconductor startups for anywhere from 10–50 cents on the dollar compared to valuations just a short while earlier. Johnson & Johnson acquired drug-discovery company 3-D

Pharmaceutical for $88 million in late 2002, for example. Even though 3-D now had more time-tested science and drug discovery in progress, just a couple years earlier its less mature R&D easily could have cost Johnson & Johnson two or three times as much. Not that the risk and uncertainty of R&D by M&A was gone by any means, but the risk/reward ratio seemed slightly more rational.

Similarly, to help fill out its wireless technology and product portfolio, RF Micro Devices acquired privately held semiconductor startups RF Nitro and Resonext in late 2001 and 2002, respectively. Despite being a far from certain bet, Resonext did already have some products and customers. RF Nitro's technology was an even earlier-stage bet, but promised potentially radical performance improvements in semiconductor technology. Neither purchase was a fire-sale bargain. Even in a down overall market, wireless remained a relatively hot sector. Still, the startups' price tags seemed more reasonable at about $1.9 million per engineer instead of the peak M&A technology market prices of $19 million or more per engineer (that is, if anyone still gave any credence to such curious metrics).

In 2004, Cisco itself aggressively re-entered the innovation-by-acquisition game with a renewed—though also much recalibrated—strategy. Shopping around for new technologies and new markets was back in style, yet the terms differed this time around. Prices for hot young startups with the promise of great new things ran more in the $80 million, rather than $8 billion, range. Talk about relative bargains: Venture capitalists had plowed more than $250 million into Procket Networks's R&D since 1999, but Cisco paid just $89 million (in cash, not stock) for the assets of the core router hardware and software maker in June 2004. A month later, Cisco paid just $9 million for control of Parc Technologies, a networking technology startup whose earlier second-round of venture funding had totaled $23 million.

With due diligence—at the right price and with the right risk/reward ratio—and with a good plan for integration, acquiring even uncertain, early stage R&D or potentially fickle innovation talent can still be a reasonable, and sometimes even an exceptional, bet. In contrast, later stage, more product-driven acquisitions (post-commercialization) offer a different, less uncertain proposition. In either case, however, smart deals can be done.

A Durable Part of a Core Innovation Strategy

The excesses and errors of the innovation-by-acquisition binge must not be allowed to obscure the fact that many companies have been able to use innovation acquisitions in a successful and sustainable fashion. In most of these cases, M&A have functioned not primarily as substitutes or replacements for core innovation, but rather as a unique means to renew, supplement, or reorient a firm's innovation focus in a steady and measured way. To this end, innovation by acquisition offers possibilities that the other innovation modes (venturing, licensing, and partnering) cannot match. Beyond any existing products or assets that might be purchased, only M&A can bring a rich new mix of high-potential talent and technologies directly to an acquirer. The great potential value can only be realized, of course, if due diligence is done well, if the price is right, and if the talent and technology can be integrated successfully.[17] These remain the core challenges.

Even while Cisco received most of the attention, for example, IBM more quietly used M&A to transform its innovation focus. In a relatively gradual but significant series of acquisitions, IBM successfully reoriented toward less reliance on hardware and greater competence in software and services. IBM did not abandon its prolific hardware competencies. Instead, its string of software and services acquisitions helped supplement, and shift over time, the innovation center-of-gravity of the entire company. The acquired companies tended to be up-and-coming leaders in software and services, already with proven technologies and significant and growing sales. They brought with them more than just products. They also brought a potential fountain of new talent and technologies. In regard to one key acquisition, for example, "The union of IBM and systems management company Tivoli Systems . . . has surprised skeptics. Rather than seeing its innovation crushed by IBM's once-domineering corporate culture . . . Tivoli took the development reins."[18] This was a recurring pattern. Cumulatively, and with the complementary realignment of its own internal R&D initiatives, IBM's acquisitions were an effective way to reorient and then refocus its innovation core.

To this end, IBM addressed the critical intangible issues relatively successfully. It persuaded key people to stay engaged and keep the acquired firms' innovation churning. To achieve greater integration, IBM often let the acquired talents and cultures take charge, rather than the other way around. The more acquired innovation is dependent on intangibles, the more these sorts of "softer" things—not golden handcuffs—are key to make the integration of talent and technologies work. At least initially, some quibbled with the prices and purpose of IBM's acquisitions. They certainly did not transform the $80 billion behemoth into a fast-growth company overnight. But by most reasonable standards, IBM dramatically improved the payoff on these investments through both deft integration and by smartly leveraging these new technologies and talents to power forward its other core businesses.

Other firms in a wide variety of industries have pursued similar paths: GE Medical Systems, Johnson & Johnson, Medtronic, and even Microsoft. These approaches are grounded primarily in post-commercialization or combination deals (i.e., acquiring established high-tech products and businesses, even if a good chunk of R&D in process and innovative talent still is a key part of the mix). With greater emphasis on proven technologies and real businesses, these strategies are more akin to traditional M&A transactions. More conventional strategic tools and established metrics better apply and they might seem less risky. It's worth remembering, however, that the majority of even more "traditional" M&A stumble. Like any other approach, innovation by acquisition is a gamble. It's always a matter of doing as much as possible to better the odds. Over time, with sound strategies, reasonable prices, and effective integration, M&A can build a solid record of innovation success.

In contrast to more mature and evolutionary innovation-by-acquisition approaches, the upheaval of more radical and trans-formative R&D-oriented deals tends to cause greater problems. It is a daunting challenge to try to transform a company's innovation core suddenly and dramatically. Widespread internal strategic and organizational difficulties compound with technological and market uncertainty to make for unfavorable odds. Monsanto's attempt to switch rapidly from old-line chemicals to newfangled agricultural biotechnology stumbled in the late 1990s, for example. Its attempt at radical transformation through a series of rapid acquisitions turned out to be too far and too fast a leap into the unknown.

Limits of Innovation by Acquisition

The experience of King Pharmaceuticals also highlights the potential, and the limits, of innovation by acquisition. In its first decade, King made little investment in its own drug discovery and development. Instead, the firm was built almost exclusively by buying relatively minor, neglected products that no longer fit the portfolios of the ever-expanding big brand-name pharmaceutical companies. With massive drug industry consolidation and restructuring during the late 1990s, King snatched up products cast off from the likes of Bristol Myers, GlaxoSmithKline, and Johnson & Johnson. It paid relatively modest prices, sometimes as little as one or two times sales. King then reformulated the drugs, rejuvenated them, repackaged them, and remarketed them, often dramatically boosting sales and profits.

It wasn't the most high-tech, cutting-edge product development strategy, but it offered significant value-added innovation in its own relatively unique way. When King acquired the antihypertensive Altace from Aventis in 1998, for example, sales were just $92 million. By 2002, King boosted Altace sales to half a billion dollars. Using this bargain acquisition-and-repackaging strategy, King built a billion-dollar company in just a few short years.

Still, the novelty of King's strategy began to wear thin before long. Confronting a series of patent expirations and new generic competitors was bad enough. Perhaps worse was that, by now, others had noticed King's once-novel R&D by M&A strategy and had moved to replicate its success. With more competitive bidding and higher prices for secondary drugs being shed by Big Pharma, King was forced to reconsider its strategy. Without its own strong R&D or drug pipeline, it was unclear how much (or whether) King had any distinct and sustainable advantage with which to defend and grow its targeted markets profitably.

King had to decide whether to strategically shift its focus and invest a great deal more in its own internal R&D and other new sources of drug development, or to take the chance and rely on others to provide it with a continuing stream of product. Both options presented greater risks and costs going forward. Burdened with such a difficult choice and with its performance sagging because of its most recent pricier drug deals, King agreed to be acquired by Mylan Laboratories in mid 2004.

The bottom line is that it's extremely difficult to build a sustainable and lucrative innovation strategy solely, or even primarily, by acquisition. There's no guarantee that the key innovations a firm needs can or will be developed by someone else, that they'll be on the market when they're needed (if ever), and that they won't be either pre-emptively snatched up by another firm or else bid up by competitors to a price that captures or exceeds all the innovation's potential future value. These are some of the key, persistent problems with the use of acquisitions, however attractive the just-buy-it philosophy seems in the abstract. A firm's core innovation assets are the leverage with which acquisitions' value can be uniquely enhanced and multiplied, even in excess of rich purchase prices. In contrast, too much reliance on acquisitions, and a corresponding lack of core innovation, tends to put a firm in a weaker, more dependent, and less profitable position.

M&A have become an increasingly important innovation option, including even for more basic R&D tasks. Sometimes, M&A are an essential and irreplaceable tool. In the end, however, innovation by acquisition is an incomplete and imperfect approach (see Table 5-1). Even the most successful and diverse examples, from Cisco Systems to King Pharmaceuticals, show not only its potential, but also its costs, risks, and limitations. Rarely are M&A alone a sustainable and lucrative innovation strategy. It takes more than just the art of the deal.

Table 5-1 Innovation by Acquisition: Just Buy It?

	The Promise/The Theory	**The Problem/The Reality**
The Deal	Acquire innovation quickly: Be first or at least fast to deal. Benefits of speed outweigh the costs, good targets won't wait. Acquire best R&D in the open market, tap startups' strengths. Need to use more strategic valuation methods, comparables.	Rushed deals, weak buyer negotiating positions, limited due diligence, too-high prices, risk/reward imbalance. Speed is no guarantee of success. Almost any valuation can be justified with newfangled logics, comparables, "it's just stock" notion.

(continued)

Table 5-1 Innovation by Acquisition: Just Buy It? (*continued*)

	The Promise/The Theory	**The Problem/The Reality**
	Use stock to pay, it's just paper money, no real cash impact, eases high purchase prices. What will our stock do if we *don't* aggressively acquire innovation?	Deals and pricing become self-justifying "at any cost." Whether stock or cash, $1 of value = $1. Write downs and losses. Buyers tend to rush in and buy high, but get skittish and bypass R&D bargains when prices drop.
The Technology	Need for acquiring innovation now—will take too long, be too slow to develop internally. Get radical, cutting-edge, world-class R&D—we couldn't develop it in-house if we wanted. "Outsource" our R&D labs, buy earlier and earlier stage R&D. Fill out holes in the technology portfolio, gain key pieces of the puzzle.	Rushed deals, limited or poor due diligence of unfamiliar R&D, technologies, and capabilities. Buy raw, premature, unproven assets, including big duds and lemons. Slow: problems and delays integrating acquired R&D, talent, and assets with existing technologies and products. Undue reliance on M&A can ultimately leave a firm weaker, more dependent, and less profitable.
The Talent	We don't have the internal expertise to develop all the innovation that's needed. It's too slow and piecemeal to hire and nurture individual talent. Acquire the best and brightest technical, creative, and entrepreneurial talent *en masse*. The talent and teams alone are worth rich prices. Use golden handcuffs, such as stock and options or phased bonuses, to retain and motivate talent long after the deal is done.	Top talent walks out the door soon after the deal is done; the best leave first. High-performing teams tend to stick together—including when they leave! Golden handcuffs often don't work. Top talent wants freedom and has plenty of opportunity elsewhere. The acquisition deal gives them money and credibility to leave and start their next venture. Incumbent talent resents the remaining "nouveau riche" acquired talent and fumes or departs.

6

SPINNOVATION
Liberating Value or Spinning Out of Control?

"By combining the entrepreneurial atmosphere of a startup venture with the financial and managerial strengths of a large, well-established company, I believe we have created a new kind of corporate enterprise."

—George Hatsopoulos

Most of the other newfangled approaches to innovation (e.g., corporate venturing and R&D by M&A) focused on aggressively attempting to bring more innovation *inside* the firm. The explicit idea of the spinout was far different. The objective and method of the spinout was to cast bigger and better innovations *outside* the parent organization. Spin out even the best and most promising core innovations to set them free and let them flourish.[1] Spinouts proliferated as offspring

of everything from retail consumer firms to old-line industrial equipment makers. Corporate dot-com spinouts became the most common
expression of the idea, but they were hardly the only type or form.

A spinout required the creation of a separate firm, a new company legally and organizationally distinct from its parent. The spinout would have its own formal and independent incorporation,
board of directors, management team, financial statements, and equity. A spinout's key distinguishing feature was that it was clearly a
distinct corporate entity, not just another corporate division or subsidiary of the parent.

The idea of *spinnovation* was still largely a curiosity even by the
mid 1990s. The concept really took off as the technology boom and
frenzied financial markets encouraged the birth of numerous high-tech
corporate offspring during the latter half of the decade. The basic thinking was that successful development and commercialization of corporate innovation required new and different types of organizations and
new and different types of organizational structures, ones that went
even far beyond simple corporate venturing. With corporate venturing,
the buck (literally and figuratively) still stopped with the corporate
parent. However creatively structured, internal corporate ventures ultimately reported to the top of the company's chain of command and
depended on the budgets and blessings of corporate headquarters.

Liberating Innovation?

Spinouts offered a better, more liberated solution. A successful innovation organization didn't have to just *act* more like a startup (an
internal corporate venture), but it had to actually *be* more like a
startup. It had to be spun out. By creating legally and organizationally separate new ventures, spinouts could liberate powerful new
ideas and high-promise ventures that ached to break free from the

stifling atmosphere of the parent company's established corporate bureaucracy. Ideally, spinouts had the best advantages of respected corporate parenting, while also having the increased freedom, focus, and motivation of a startup entrepreneurial venture.

Perhaps just as importantly, spinouts' unique organizational, legal, and financial structuring offered the opportunity for parents to raise large sums of outside capital to fund promising, but risky, ideas. Venture capital or other forms of private investment, or even the public markets directly (through an IPO), could be tapped to share the costs and risks. Moreover, compared with a typical entrepreneurial venture, raising cash would be easy. Investors would buy in quickly and contribute more with a respected corporate parent as a namesake founder, primary co-investor, and privileged nurturer of its own spinout offspring. Good parenting and pedigree conferred substantial privileges.

Spinouts offered other organizational and financial advantages. With separate, dedicated equity for the spinout, the parent and its partners could craft high-powered incentives (e.g., stock and options) for spinout managers to be more truly aggressive entrepreneurs. The stock of an old-line S&P 500 company simply couldn't compete with the potential upside of a real stake in an entrepreneurial spinout. In contrast, internal corporate venturing offered the possibility to create "phantom" stock and options at best. With a spinout, the opportunities for big-payoff financial incentives were very real and almost unlimited. These were not phantom shares; they were cold, hard, real equity. They offered a more clear, direct, and powerful fuel for entrepreneurial energies. They also offered potential currency with which to do deals or otherwise entice and enlist partners, customers, and other stakeholders.

After setting the spinout structure and process in place, corporate parents could ease back and watch their offsprings' value soar as the latent potential of previously languishing corporate innovations was unleashed. Newly focused entrepreneurial spinouts would flourish.

At the same time, by keeping significant strategic and organizational ties, as well as significant ownership stakes and other financial links to their newly spunout ventures, parent companies would still be able to realize synergies with their offspring and, ultimately, would be able to capture most of the ultimate value created.

Corporate.coms

With the advent of the Internet, spinouts seemed particularly attractive and appropriate. Established companies could spin out Internet versions of themselves to beat startups at their own game. The list of dot-com spinout ventures quickly expanded: Barnes&Noble.com, Bluelight.com (Kmart), FTD.com, McAfee.com, Playboy.com, RadioShack.com, Sales.com, Staples.com, ToysRUs.com, Walmart.com, and so on. The thinking was that the core established firms simply couldn't or shouldn't try to embrace the Internet wholly themselves. The technologies, cultures, and business models were just too different and disruptive. The parent firms simply "didn't get it"; even if they did, they were too stodgy and slow to react. Moreover, the parent companies did not always have, or want to invest, the significant capital required to take their e-commerce dreams to fruition—at least not as quickly and grandly as they needed to. Spin out a corporate dot-com, however, and analysts and investors, talent and customers, all would swoon.

Just as quickly as they had proliferated, most Internet-era spinouts quickly fizzled. They often left a trail of less-than-stellar investments and strategic, organizational, and legal complications in their wake. Typical of the other innovation fads and fashions, the promotion of spinouts as a new and uniquely powerful model for innovation continued to gain momentum even as many high-profile spinouts—including many companies featured as exemplars—already were experiencing serious difficulties. Within just a couple years, most of these innovation-driven spinouts were spun back in, sold off, or shut down.

Enduring lessons can be learned from these numerous stumbled spinouts. As with the other innovation fads and fashions, it's too easy to dismiss their rise and fall as just an inevitable function of the overall craziness of the Internet boom and bust. This is not the case. Spinouts were not only the rage for old-line companies looking to tap the power and possibilities of the Internet. Many other companies in a wide variety of industries—from industrial goods and retail to biotech and pharmaceuticals—also pursued spinnovation as a solution for their innovation challenges. From Thermo Electron to Toys R Us, the examples show that, despite their myriad theoretical and potential advantages, the promise of spinouts often falls short in practice. This does not have to be the case. Spinouts have the potential to liberate and create enormous value—if done right, and for the right reasons.

Spinning Out of Control

The recent history of Thermo Electron illustrates the dynamics and challenges of the spinnovation strategy. George Hatsopoulos, the founder of Thermo Electron, was one of the great entrepreneurs and company builders of the past few decades. Starting in 1956 with $50,000, he built Thermo Electron into one of the world's leading technical and medical equipment companies during the next 40 years. For most of its history, Thermo Electron methodically went about building its businesses, adding new technologies and divisions to its incrementally expanding corporate portfolio. It was a successful but quiet company involved in a wide variety of markets such as test, measurement, and monitoring equipment. But it was not a Wall Street darling, to say the least.

During the mid 1980s and early 1990s, Hatsopoulos embarked upon a novel strategy, one that would eventually garner more attention and much greater financial acclaim. Hatsopoulos was frustrated by the need for more capital to build Thermo Electron's technology-intensive businesses. He was also intent on fostering among his managers the same sort of entrepreneurial spirit that drove him to found Thermo Electron. To address both concerns, Thermo Electron began to spin out more and more new technologies as independent but still Thermo-affiliated companies. The flurry of offspring eventually generated more than a couple dozen spinouts, many with their own IPOs and publicly traded shares. Several of the spinouts then went on to spawn their own new technology spinouts. Thermo Electron typically maintained a majority ownership stake in its offspring and also maintained numerous other administrative, financial, and organizational ties.

The logic was simple but compelling: Leverage the incubational and operational benefits of scale and support that a large corporate parent (Thermo Electron) could provide, while simultaneously gaining the financial and entrepreneurial flexibility of focused, IPOed, new business ventures. Everyone would benefit: Thermo as the corporate parent, the spunout businesses and their managers, and outside investors and partners:

- **The Parent**—Thermo Electron would be able to independently raise capital for each of its spunout businesses. Through private fundraising and especially public equity issues (IPOs), it would be able to fund promising, but risky and capital-intensive, new technology ventures better and cheaper than it could through internal corporate funding. Thermo Electron still would reap most of the gains of any successes by maintaining a large (usually majority) stake in each of the spinouts, as well as by securing other revenue streams from its offspring through ongoing technology, marketing, and administrative affiliations.

- **The Spinout**—Managers and technical talent of the new spinout ventures would gain the liberation of entrepreneurial ownership and control that would never be possible as just another internal corporate division. Managers could make their own strategic decisions and then share in their own successes through their direct, real equity and option stakes in the spinout. Thermo Electron could thereby better attract, retain, and motivate top technical and managerial talent. At the same time, all the spinouts would continue to benefit from having the ongoing, supportive parentage and pedigree of Thermo Electron to help incubate and support their nascent technologies and businesses.

- **Investors and partners**—Investors and other potential partners could join Thermo Electron in supporting clear and focused entrepreneurial spinout ventures whose strategic and financial potential wouldn't get buried within the complexity and bureaucracy of the corporate parent. Unlike with a typical high-risk startup, investors would get the benefit of buying into more mature and developed spunout technologies that had been, and would continue to be, looked after by a respected corporate parent. Raising additional capital and dealing with the financial markets would be easier for each individual technology venture. Separate spunout businesses would provide much greater simplicity and clarity for analysts and investors alike.

In the wake of this radical and ever-expanding strategic, organizational, and financial experiment, revenues of the Thermo group grew dramatically. The market richly rewarded both the parent and its spinouts. Thermo Electron's market value tripled from 1993 to 1996. The enthusiasm for Thermo Electron's strategy was so great that a dedicated mutual fund sprouted in 1996 to try to tap into its success. The Thermo Opportunity Fund was founded to invest the majority of its assets in Thermo Electron and its various offspring. Thermo became not only a Wall Street darling, but also the focus of numerous glowing case studies and articles in both management and finance.

Thermo Electron's spinout structure seemed to offer many substantial benefits that alleviated or solved some of the key problems of corporate innovation. It was ideal in the sense that, carved out from the parent, the spinout strategies " . . . subject units of the company to the scrutiny of the capital markets, allow the compensation contracts of unit managers to be based on market performance, and shift capital acquisition and investment decisions from centralized control to unit managers."[2] Each spinout was more nimble and focused, offering great benefits to both investors and managers. At the same time, the continuing interrelationships and leverage of the overall Thermo portfolio offered ongoing benefits of synergy and diversity to each spinout, all unified by a strong common corporate parentage. It was the best of both worlds.

Another exploration of Thermo Electron's novel spinout business design offered similar observations: "From a technology company that developed and manufactured products, Thermo Electron transformed itself into a [sort of] venture capital firm that spins out promising technologies into separate units and supports those units with financial backing, technical know-how, and other business resources."[3] Thermo was now something different, something much more than just a technical and medical equipment manufacturer. Thermo Electron offered a new model for innovation: the corporate innovator as the hub of a network of aggressive, entrepreneurial spinouts. Thermo wasn't just spinning out peripheral new technologies; it was spinning out some of its best and biggest innovations.

Unraveling of the Spinouts

Even as the accolades grew and as its spinnovation began to be increasingly emulated, Thermo Electron and its investors began to have some serious doubts and second thoughts about the strategy. By 1998, they no longer saw the focus and drive of individual entrepreneurial ventures or the clear and powerful discipline of the financial markets. They woke one morning to instead see a corporate holding company at the center of a confusing constellation of two dozen partially spunout subsidiaries. Each quasi-independent spinout had its own board, meaning the entire Thermo constellation of spinouts generated more than 100 board meetings per year. Managers complained that Thermo was a series of fiefdoms and that it was often more difficult to do business with a fellow Thermo spinout than it was with a competitor. Each spinout had duplication and overlap in many basic business operations and functions. Customers and investors were confused: Who and what was Thermo Electron? The incoming president admitted that he didn't know what exactly Thermo Electron was until he was offered the job, even though he had been doing business with numerous Thermo spinouts for years.

On the financial side, many of the spinouts languished as they failed to attract and maintain sufficient levels of interest from analysts and investors to keep their stocks afloat. They simply were too small in terms of revenues and market capitalization (ranging as low as in the tens of millions) and too thinly traded to attract enough attention. Worse, analysts and investors found it increasingly difficult to make sense of Thermo Electron's complex web of strategic, organizational, and financial ties to its numerous spunout offspring. When Thermo Electron reported negative results in one of its major spinouts in early 1998, the questions and doubts grew and the parent's own stock began a deep and hard slide.

Many of the supposed benefits of Thermo's spinout strategy appeared to quickly unravel. To management and employees, analysts and investors, Thermo's constellation of spinouts had become more confusing than clear, and more cumbersome than liberating. In one year, Thermo Electron plummeted from almost $40 per share to nearly $10, even as the economy and the market continued to glow and grow. Clearly, the gloss was off Thermo's previously much celebrated example. Thermo Electron's founders retired. A new management team came on board.

Refocusing the Core

Thermo Electron's new leadership started their job by conceding that many of the company's spinouts were, in fact, core businesses that needed to be brought back more fully and formally under the corporate umbrella. Conversely, other non-core businesses needed to be fully and unequivocally divested, not just partially spun out. In January 2000, three months prior to the tech market crash, Thermo Electron announced a sweeping reorganization. The company initiated plans to buy back most of its spinout subsidiaries. Other non-core, partially spunout assets were to be wholly and completely divested.

Thermo Electron began transforming itself into a single, unified company focused on life sciences, optical technologies, and test and measurement equipment. The goal of the new strategy was to become one unified, publicly traded firm with a greatly simplified structure—to become "a highly integrated, tightly managed operating company." Thermo Electron billed its refocusing as making it "the first post-'90s company." Starkly contrary to the logic of the prior spinout-driven strategy, Chairman Richard Syron explained, "We knew that making Thermo one company focused on one industry would unlock the value within Thermo, make us competitive for the future, and position us for growth." By the end of 2001, Thermo had undone almost all of its spinouts, dramatically reversing its earlier, radical, spinnovation experiment.

Spin.com: How *Not* to Spin

Thermo Electron's spinout strategy set the model for the flurry of technology and Internet spinouts that soon followed. Yet, even as Thermo Electron's constellation of spinouts collapsed in 1998 and 1999, few outside the company seemed to notice or carefully consider Thermo's now more complicated spinout experiences. Few lessons were learned. The spinout strategy took on new glamour and urgency, as everyone from established blue-chip companies, such as Wal-Mart, Staples, Enron, and Tyco, to dot-com retailers and Internet media plays, jumped onto the spinout bandwagon. Just a few weeks after Thermo Electron announced its massive unspinning, for example, Wal-Mart announced it was partnering with VC co-investors Accel Partners to spin out a new Silicon Valley–based offspring, Walmart.com.

The vast majority of these Internet and technology spinouts just being launched would struggle with exactly the same sorts of dilemmas that had plagued Thermo Electron. Spinout stumbles followed in a wide variety of companies and industries:

- **Wal-Mart/Walmart.com**—Wal-Mart retained a majority stake, but eventually spun it back in, buying back VC-owned shares to make it a wholly owned subsidiary.

- **Kmart/Bluelight.com**—Kmart retained 60 percent, but then spun it all back in by buying back VC-owned shares to make it a wholly owned subsidiary.

- **Staples/Staples.com**—Staples retained 82.5 percent, but then reversed a planned spinout IPO; it bought back VC and employee shares to make the dot-com a wholly owned subsidiary.

- **FTD/FTD.com**—FTD retained 98 percent of voting stock, but then spun the dot-com back in entirely by buying back its public shares, saying FTD.com was "too small a company to move forward" on its own.

- **Network Associates/McAfee.com**—Network Associates retained 85 percent, with 95 percent voting shares, then down to 75 percent, but spun the entire thing in, buying back all publicly held shares to make it a wholly owned subsidiary.

- **Nordstrom/Nordstrom.com**—Nordstrom retained a majority stake, but then spun it all back in by buying back outside investors' shares to make it a wholly owned subsidiary.

- **Playboy/Playboy.com**—Playboy planned an IPO for its dot-com offspring, but canceled it at the last minute; Playboy.com instead became a new corporate division.

- **Siebel Systems/Sales.com**—Siebel retained a big minority stake, but the entire venture was shut down in July 2001; Siebel Systems launched its own internal Internet division in 2003.

- **RadioShack/RadioShack.com**—RadioShack retained 75 percent, but then spun it all back in by buying back the 25 percent outside interest.

- **Toys R Us/ToysRUs.com**—Toys R Us retained a majority stake, but a deal with VC partners was subsequently withdrawn and the dot-com venture instead became a wholly owned subsidiary.

It wasn't just corporate dot-coms, either. Other examples ranged from pharmaceuticals to utilities to fiber optics:

- **ICN/Ribapharm**—ICN initially retained 80 percent, but then spun it all back in by buying back all publicly held shares to make it a wholly owned subsidiary.

- **Enron/Azurix**—Enron retained 67 percent, but then spun it back in entirely by buying back all publicly held shares.

- **Tyco/Tycom**—Tyco retained 86 percent, but then spun it back in entirely by buying back all publicly held shares to make it a wholly owned subsidiary.

In examining the history of dozens of other cases of spinnovation, the overall record was mixed and often disappointing. Many were plagued by difficulties from the start (see Table 6-1). The initial difficulties and failed or spun-in spinouts all tended to share one or more (often all) of the following common problems:

- **The crown jewels spinout**—Innovation assets too close to the parent's core were spun out, often followed by regret, reconsideration, and eventually attempted "recall" of the spinout. But undoing a spinout might not be a simple transaction at all—including legally, organizationally, and financially. A spinout might seem the best way to provide the clarity and focus needed for a large and established firm to grow some of its most promising new ventures, even its core innovations. A spinout might appear to offer a more entrepreneurial structure and culture, as well as new capital and fresh equity, not available when innovation remains buried within a corporate bureaucracy. Before long, however, many parents fret that they might have spun out some of their crown jewels. After this realization hits, it's not always easy or cheap to buy them back. From Old Economy R&D spinouts to the myriad corporate Internet dot-com offspring, this is a common spinnovation dilemma.

- **The one-legged stool spinout**—The spinout could not stand on its own terms and could not gain traction as an independent operating business. Companies might try to spin out embryonic, partially formed ideas and inventions that have limited coherence and shaky standalone business models. A premature idea or a mere piece of a business model (such as some raw, basic science or a single sales channel) is usually not a good foundation for a successful, standalone spinout. Most of the corporate Internet dot-coms fell victim to this problem: Bluelight.com, FTD.com, McAfee.com, Nordstrom.com, Playboy.com, RadioShack.com, Staples.com, ToysRUs.com, Walmart.com, and others. A successful spinout should have a credible independent business case in terms of strategy, operations, and finances. If it doesn't, the parent needs to decide whether to simply re-integrate the innovation into its own core businesses or to invest what might be considerable time and resources to nurture it further so that it might be later spun out. Alternately, the parent might try to partner, license, or sell the innovation to let someone else incubate it further, or just simply shelf the idea altogether.

- **The piggy-bank spinout**—Another common problem was the piggy-bank spinout. The spinout was primarily motivated by short-term financial exigencies or accounting gimmickry, such as the desire to goose financial statements by getting rid of expenses and debt or to raise quick cash, instead of building a sound long-term strategy. In many new business ventures, capital requirements are large, the risk is substantial, and the payoffs can be relatively distant. The parent firm might be hesitant to commit large resources to a new venture, even if it looks like a core investment. The corporate parent might be more concerned about quarterly earnings reports or other short-term financial exigencies. Raising capital externally through a spinout therefore proves to be alluring. But myopic financial gimmickry can create more problems than it solves if it's used only to avoid (or, more likely, simply delay) the pain and responsibility of tough investment choices. Over time, purely financial-driven spinout decisions aggravate numerous tensions, including conflicts of interest for the parent, spinout, and investors alike. Many of Enron's infamous spinouts, from new utility companies to new Internet ventures, and others, such as Tyco's Tycom spinout, fell into this category. In smaller or much less scandalous ways, so did many other technology and non-technology spinouts alike (for example, ICN-Ribapharm and many corporate dot-coms).

All the above problems tend to interact and compound each other. The vast array of retail spinouts, such as Walmart.com, Bluelight.com, and Staples.com, were born of Internet euphoria, when it seemed that the web would transform retailing and leave brick-and-mortar retailers in the dust. Promoters extolled the benefits of spinouts as a way both to externally raise quick cash and to respond in a fast and entrepreneurial way. Soon enough, however, ill-formed Internet-retailing business models struggled on small volumes to support their own marketing, operations, finance, human resources, distribution, and fulfillment efforts. Both Walmart.com and Bluelight.com were bought back and spun in by their corporate parents less than 18 months after being spun out.

Staples.com was one of the more initially successful online-retail efforts. However, parent Staples's plans to spin out Staples.com and do an IPO were cut short as the spinout's foggy strategic and financial rationale quickly evaporated. Instead, Staples.com was pulled back and folded into Staples's core business. Reversing their earlier thinking, Staples's executives now noted that Staples.com indeed was an integral part of, and key channel for, the parent firm's core business. Even simply stopping the Staples.com spinout-in-process created problems. Some Staples shareholders revolted and filed suit as the parent tried to buy back Staples.com executives' pre-IPO equity of the now-defunct spinout at what were viewed as unfairly inflated prices.

189

Table 6-1 Liberating Value or Spinning Out of Control?

	The Promise/The Theory	The Problem/The Reality
Internal Strategic and Organizational Issues: Focus and Autonomy	The spinout will be its own company and organization, free to act nimbly and do what's best strategically. The spinout will have its own unique and clear focus. Innovation will not get lost or quashed in the parent company's complexity and bureaucracy. The spinout will have a new and more liberated innovation culture. Leadership and top talent will be better attracted and motivated to "run their own show." The spinout will still benefit from its pedigreed parentage and ongoing corporate ties and synergies. Spinouts therefore make sense for both "excess" innovation and even (or especially) core innovation.	The shadow of the corporate parent lingers—it maintains majority ownership, executive and/or board domination, and complicated and onerous ties with its offspring. Autonomy may be a ruse—the spinout is hamstrung, second-guessed, or quietly vetoed by the parent. The spinout nonetheless tries its best to "do its own thing," often duplicating or working at odds with the parent's own efforts and investments; even greater tensions and conflicts may arise. The result: problems from the beginning, hampered strategy, execution, and performance. Complicated spin-ins or even failure. Spinouts can distract or detract from the parent firm's core innovation needs and challenges. Companies might mistakenly carve out and pawn off their future.
External Stakeholder and Financial Issues: Funding and Partners	Real spinout equity and options are created to help motivate and retain spinout leadership and other talent. The spinout can strike new and better partnerships, strategically and financially, after its corporate parent frees it. Investors will line up to fund a promising new spinout that has the nurturing and strong backing of an established corporate parent. A spinout is the best way to liberate innovation's value and maximize value creation for both core and non-core innovation.	Tensions and problems can arise from using the parent's corporate assets to enrich a few spinout elite. Potential partners might be spooked by lingering parent-spinout ties. Investors might shy away or demand preferential terms because of perceived parent-spinout conflicts of interest, including onerous contracts and other side agreements, royalties, restrictions, and so on. Ill-formed spinouts are set up to stumble from the start, end up subtracting value. Spinouts can distract, detract from core innovation; parent loses value.

The Umbilical-Cord Spinout

What Thermo Electron, the myriad dot-com corporate spinouts, and so many other spinouts also have in common is an "umbilical cord" dilemma. The parent company cannot bring itself to sever its continuing ties of ownership and control with its own offspring. The parent might be reluctant to let go because the business really shouldn't have been spun out in the first place. Or, the parent simply might not want to share too much of the spinout "pie" with outside partners and investors. To try to better profit from the spinout, for example, parents often press onerous conditions on their offspring: high royalty payments, restrictive and expensive licenses, exorbitant management fees, guaranteed buyer/supplier contracts, and so on. As a result, the too-close, continuing corporate relationship smothers or strangles the fledgling spinout. Ultimately, the ties that bind can cause strategic, organizational, legal, and financial difficulties for the parent as well.

Whatever the reasoning and objectives, a partial "umbilical cord" spinout is often little more than another subsidiary of the parent; many relevant stakeholders perceive it as exactly that. Any sort of quasi-autonomy given to a spinout under these conditions is, at best, a weak substitute for true independence and, at worst, is simply a ruse. Continuing entanglements with the parent firm are likely to interfere with effective decision making for the spinout, which to succeed needs to truly chart its own course. At the same time, the lingering shadow of the parent can spook key outside stakeholders, particularly potential partners and investors. The variety of tensions and conflicts that result can cause considerable complications for both spinout and parent.

The spinout of Barnes&Noble.com reveals some of these inherent complexities. After Barnes & Noble took public one-fourth of the dot-com spinout in 1999, shares briefly bumped up, but then slid down from an offering price of $18 to less than $1 over the next couple years. Barnes & Noble eventually decided to buy back the dot-com shares and make the spinout a full subsidiary. The reasons? To cut combined costs (not just operating costs, but also the costs of administering two separate public companies) and to strengthen the Barnes & Noble brand. Barnes & Noble initially offered $2.50 per share. The offer was quickly followed by more than a dozen lawsuits charging that the deal was "inadequate and constitutes unfair dealing." The suits alleged that Barnes & Noble had unfairly abused its dominant stake and "breached its duty" to Barnes&Noble.com shareholders. Barnes & Noble upped its offer and settled the suits, completing the spin-in in early 2004. These types of entanglements are only some of the more visible symptoms of the more fundamental burdens—strategic, organizational, legal, and financial—under which many spinouts labor.

Navigating a Spinout

Despite the numerous possible pitfalls, spinouts—done right and for the right reasons—still offer the potential of maximizing value creation from innovation. This includes not only for the parent and spinout, but also for outside partners, investors, and other stakeholders. Innovations that might have died on the vine or simply languished inside the corporate parent can instead be brought more quickly and fully to fruition. This is especially the case for *non-core,* but still potentially valuable, innovations. From initial consideration and throughout implementation, however, spinouts present a series of critical decision points and execution hurdles. Spinouts necessitate a strategy process in which parents initially must invest and take charge. But sooner rather than later, the parents need to step back, let go, and refocus on their own core businesses, even as the spinout is set free to chart its own course.

The story of Targacept, Inc. provides a good illustration of how, when, and why spinouts can fit into the innovation mix. Targacept, a development-stage pharmaceutical firm, was spun out from R.J. Reynolds Tobacco Company. Targacept's journey illustrates not only the uses and challenges of the spinout strategy, it also highlights some of the key issues raised by all the other innovation approaches discussed thus far—i.e., the inherent problems of corporate venturing, the limitations of IP licensing, the difficulties of partnering, and the dilemmas of innovation by acquisition.

Corporate Venturing and Innovation Spillovers

Innovation is not a defined and predictable endeavor; a tremendous amount of creativity, serendipity, and unintended discovery is inherently involved. Consequently, in the process of substantially and continually investing in R&D and new business development, firms are likely to have significant innovation spillovers. They might find a lot of what they weren't necessarily looking for in the first place. Other times, a firm's initial innovation goals can be both clear and achieved, but time and circumstances might have diminished their relevance and attractiveness for the parent firm's now-evolved strategy. A company might face the dilemma of having a plethora of potentially valuable innovation assets that no one knows what to do with. This problem of excess innovation is especially prevalent inside larger companies, with sometimes dozens of different R&D programs and enormous annual research and new business development expenditures. Xerox and Lucent are two key examples of this (see Chapter 2).

The problem of excess innovation also happens in some of the most unlikely places. In the early 1980s, the leadership of R.J. Reynolds Tobacco (RJR) made a strategic decision to invest in a strong focus on science. The idea was that RJR should be the world's leader in understanding nicotine and related issues—the pharmacology, the chemistry, and the toxicology. Top management believed it would help develop safer products and help better address controversial issues, such as addiction. Much like many other R&D skunkworks and corporate-venturing initiatives, the Nicotine Research and Analogue Development Program (NRADP) was well funded and set loose.

For nearly 15 years, RJR devoted millions of dollars to fund NRADP. A rich talent pool and world-class research programs grew. The operation was run much like a research institute, with an environment as much academic as business. A lot of far-reaching basic R&D, in which a company might not normally invest, took root. The labs were incubating new ideas, patents, and technologies, and evermore derivatives of each. Eventually, some researchers began to realize that the discoveries for which they had labored so long and so hard might actually have some commercial applications. One serendipitous discovery was that many of the compounds that NRADP scientists were working with seemed to have potential applications to alleviate a wide variety of ailments: Alzheimer's disease, pain, depression, schizophrenia, Parkinson's disease, ulcerative colitis, attention deficit disorder, Tourette's syndrome, obesity, and other problems especially related to the brain and central nervous system.

At the same time, scientists outside RJR were noting that tobacco users had reduced susceptibility to, and symptoms of, many such ailments. Nicotine appeared to be one common reason why. Although nicotine is quite toxic and has many negative side effects, in small dosages it might also have notable beneficial effects. Some of RJR's researchers began to explore how and why beneficial effects existed. They also focused more on exploring how the negative side effects of nicotine could be greatly diminished or even eliminated by creating entirely new but similar-acting compounds. Nicotinic-based compounds had the ability to "tune" the brain and central nervous system.

Cigarettes and Pharmaceuticals Don't Mix

Despite the NRADP's scientific progress, RJR's R&D skunkworks began to encounter difficulties. By the mid 1990s, top executives of RJR and its parent, RJR Nabisco Holdings, could no longer afford to spend their limited time, attention, and resources on some of the company's more promising, if surprising, new ventures. RJR Nabisco Holdings was in the middle of its own conglomerate breakup. Moreover, as heavy political and legal pressure on the tobacco industry mounted, RJR itself had to retrench and refocus on running its core operating businesses. Years and millions of R&D investment and some fantastically promising discoveries now just seemed to be off purpose. NRADP had some potential blockbuster innovations that nonetheless were largely irrelevant to the other huge and more immediate strategic problems RJR confronted. Corporate interest in and funding for NRADP suddenly evaporated.

Originally, NRADP's proponents had wanted to leverage its discoveries to transform the whole of RJR itself into a different kind of company. This ambitious agenda withered in the face of organizational, industry, financial, political, and legal realities. Although only a few years earlier it had been the focus of corporate R&D, NRADP was now out of fashion and out of favor in a company with many more pressing priorities. Continuing to fund and develop NRADP within RJR appeared to be a quixotic battle.

It's a common and vexing corporate-venturing problem; NRADP just didn't fit the more immediate core challenges of the parent firm. RJR's main business revolved around a simply manufactured agricultural product rolled in paper. An R&D-intensive pharmaceutical business was hardly a strategic fit with a huge cigarette business. Continuing to invest in NRADP no longer made sense.

NRADP faced extinction. Although many executives saw the latent value of its R&D, they simply could not justify supporting it any further. Some executives wanted the research program abruptly cut off and shut down altogether. Others were content to quietly extinguish it. RJR CEO Andy Schindler noted, "The scientists were enthused about the potential. But, there was no clear path to fruition for RJR."

Considering the Alternatives

Still others thought that RJR should at least try to sell or license NRADP's intellectual property portfolio to earn some nominal payback. The limited value of the raw intellectual property proved a problem. NRADP's compounds were still a long way from being tested, developed, and proven as safe and effective therapeutic drugs. Sale or license of the intellectual property would bring in only thousands of dollars, not millions. As one executive later noted, "[T]he intellectual property was not worth much, had no real, significant monetary value. We would've gotten almost nothing if we had just tried to license or sell the raw science." It was hardly worth the effort and expense.

Innovation by acquisition also proved an infeasible option. In RJR's strategic and financial predicament, it was not at all practical to try to acquire more pharmaceutical R&D and drug development assets to try to push NRADP's discoveries further toward commercialization. The idea was surfaced, but quickly scuttled. It would be hugely expensive, take far too long to bear fruit (6–8 years minimum), and pull RJR only farther from its core, cash-generating businesses into unknown territory. RJR CEO Schindler explained, "If we had followed a go-it-alone path and had tried to develop this internally [within RJR], I think we would've failed. We had no sense of the end game as a tobacco company." Neither would investors have the patience or understanding for such a move. RJR had neither the luxuries of cash and time nor the competence and capabilities to try to transform itself into a pharmaceutical company.

Partnering seemed the next logical option to consider. But pursuing an alliance or joint venture raised its own dilemmas. As

NRADP's scientists communicated their discoveries with their Big Pharma colleagues, great initial interest and enthusiasm grew. NRADP's targets and compounds offered novel approaches to try to tackle an entire series of prevalent, debilitating central nervous system conditions. After executives at one interested Big Pharma firm realized that they were talking to, and potentially collaborating with, a tobacco company, however, the discussions abruptly cooled. RJR carried considerable baggage. A joint venture or another form of ongoing collaboration did not seem a viable long-term option.

Launching a Spinout

Before making a final decision on simply shutting down NRADP, RJR brought in an outside advisor to help it surface and assess any other alternatives. A different approach was proposed, a more involved process designed to eventually spin out NRADP as an independent firm. NRADP met the strategic criteria as a good candidate for a spinout. It was no longer part of a core R&D or new business development initiative for RJR. Still, RJR's years of investment had given it solid and diverse assets to try to flourish as an independent venture. The spinout wouldn't be a "one-legged stool." It wasn't a single patent or idea, but an entire functioning group of productive resources: myriad patents, researchers, technologies, and capabilities. Moreover, a spinout offered much greater upside than any of the other options, at least if it succeeded. A bit more investment and patience would be required. Pursuing a spinout was definitely not the easiest and quickest option, but it appeared to be the best (if not the only) way to eventually realize any of NRADP's latent value.

RJR's situation highlights the balancing act of pursuing a spinout strategy. A prospective spinout-in-process must somehow survive and be nurtured as part of the parent even as it needs to plan and begin to implement its own course toward independence. The parent firm cannot afford to waste undue time, attention, and resources on executing the spinout. After all, the parent's decision to spin it out inherently suggests that it's no longer a core strategic concern.

For RJR, it was a tough trick. RJR's total R&D budget had been cut by more than half; NRADP's funding dried up. Yet, it needed millions to continue R&D. RJR CEO Schindler told NRADP's leaders it would be shut down by the end of 1998. After some heated discussions, a deal was struck: NRADP would get no more money after the year's end, but it would not be shut down. NRADP would get a chance to make a go of it, if it could figure out how to bootstrap its own support.

The spinout idea offered one possible solution. If NRADP could find outside partners and investors to facilitate the process, it might actually have a chance. RJR CEO Schindler explained his skeptical, tough-love approach, "By threatening to shut it down, I was trying to spur it to the next step. They needed that pressure; this is the kind of pressure that a new venture needs to succeed anyway."

The Process of Breaking Free

The NRADP team had to push to define the spinout's focus and purpose. It could not survive on its own as a loose gaggle of quasi-academic researchers. It had to define a vision, mission, scope, goals, and objectives as a would-be independent company. The decision was made to leverage NRADP's core patents and capabilities focusing on the brain and central nervous system. The group also brainstormed a corporate identity and name: Targacept, stemming from its R&D focus on targeting key nerve receptors. Without a well-defined strategy and purpose of its own, a fledgling spinout cannot build a credible standalone business case.

A lack of defined strategic scope and direction for a spinout can also create major conflicts between the spinout and its parent down the road. These "turf" battles can endanger a spinout's chances of success and, as the previous examples highlighted, create complex legal, strategic, and financial headaches for the parent. If the parent has serious hesitations about surrendering too much territory and freedom to its proposed spinout, it might be reason to re-examine whether a spinout is a good idea in the first place. Onerous restrictions and conditions on the spinout ultimately tend to be deleterious to both the parent and offspring.

Fortunately for Targacept, the territorial boundaries between RJR and its proposed spinout were fairly clear cut. It was unlikely that RJR would anytime soon develop a renewed interest in pharmaceutical R&D. Therefore, the more detailed process of legally, organizationally, and financially extricating Targacept from RJR got underway. RJR established Targacept as an independent subsidiary company with its own employees, assets, and financial statements. Fortunately for Targacept, RJR avoided the all-too-frequent "umbilical cord" dilemma and instead outright assigned all the core intellectual property wholly and clearly to Targacept.

Partners and Investors as Validation

Parents need to step back for their own good and for the good of the spinout. Outside partners and investors need to begin to play more of a major role, helping a spinout advance farther along in the process of gaining functional independence. Active outside partners and investors also provide critical validation for the entire concept of a spinout. If a spinout cannot attract substantial, credible, and committed outside partners and investors, it's usually a sign that the choice of a spinout strategy is flawed. It might not be a valid or sufficiently incubated concept. As RJR CEO Schindler noted, "We needed outside investment from serious partners as validation for what we had. They [pharmaceutical firms and VC investors] know the business much better than I did."

In early 1998, the new (but still 100 percent RJR-owned) Targacept subsidiary made overtures to a U.S.–based pharmaceutical giant, seeking research funding and collaboration to keep from being shut down. Negotiations proceeded smoothly and the possibility of a rewarding partnership looked promising. However, when senior executives of the promising pharmaceutical partner became aware of RJR's role, negotiations abruptly ended. Again, they hesitated to partner with a tobacco company.

As in so many spinout situations, Targacept's lingering corporate parentage, though initially providing the substantial benefits that only a generous corporate parent can provide, had now become a liability. Targacept learned its lesson. By the end of 1998, Targacept committed to a full spinout and struck a funding deal with drug giant Rhone-Poulenc Rorer to jointly explore therapies for Parkinson's and Alzheimer's diseases.

Targacept's dealings with outside investors also highlighted the need to be free. One interested VC stressed, "I am going to cut to the bottom of this: We have got to cut RJR below 50 percent. I am not going into a company where RJR has the majority of the shares." RJR agreed to take a step back and to lower its proposed stake. The leadership of both RJR and Targacept realized that RJR's stepping down to a minority role was necessary to give Targacept the best chance to succeed. Potential investors liked the fact that RJR had already assigned all the relevant IP wholly to Targacept rather than forcing the spinout to license patents and technologies and pay royalties to its parent, as is so often the practice.

Avoiding the Ties That Bind

In many spinouts, a strong tendency exists for the parent to covetously maintain majority ownership and board control. Despite RJR's loss of control, it seemed the right thing to do to give Targacept the best start. RJR CEO Schindler notes, "We decided to give up a lot of the ownership in order to increase the odds of success." Upon independence, only two of Targacept's seven board members remained RJR executives. The rest were experienced professionals with broad and deep ties to the biotechnology, pharmaceutical, and investor communities.

A spinout majority-owned and -controlled by its parent isn't really a spinout to most outside stakeholders, including key potential partners and investors. To them, it's more of a subsidiary in disguise. It's often in everyone's best interests for the parent to loosen its grip. Few savvy outsiders are likely to participate in a spinout in which they know their interests, and their investments, are subordinate to the whims of a potentially malingering corporate parent.

Relaxing the ties that bind (especially ownership and control) can create a bigger pie for everyone. By its full independence in August 2000, Targacept had raised $30.4 million in venture capital funding, one of the largest first rounds of VC funding for a biotechnology or pharmaceutical company that year. Securing these essential funds would have been more difficult, if not impossible, if Targacept had not been set forth on its own clearly independent path apart from RJR. The intangibles of independence were just as important. One scientist who joined the company noted, "I was intrigued by the notion of going to work for a promising biotech start-up, but never in a million years would I have dreamed of working for a tobacco company."

With drug development well underway on a variety of fronts, Targacept raised its second round of funding in early 2003. In a seriously down market, both overall and for biotechnology, the $60 million infusion was one of the larger VC rounds that year. Targacept also renewed, and initiated new, co-development partnerships. It even embarked on making small, targeted acquisitions of compounds related to its own unique competencies and that complemented its own compounds under development. By 2004, drug development was well underway for compounds to treat memory and cognitive disorders, Alzheimer's disease, ADHD, anxiety and depression, ulcerative colitis, pain, and other ailments. A final twist was that Targacept even began to consider whether to spin out its own powerful and proprietary computational drug discovery technologies or instead keep them inside as core assets.

Bettering the Odds of Value Creation

A spinout is not always the right way to develop and commercialize innovation. Moreover, spinouts offer many challenges in implementation. Sometimes, just killing the nascent venture is the right thing to do; the costs of pursuing other options can exceed any likely benefits. Sometimes, licensing or selling the ideas and technologies can help a company realize some small returns. Other times, joint venturing can work—for example, if it's either an innovation asset in which the parent needs to maintain a stake, or even using a JV as a prelude and preparation for a full spinout. In Targacept's case, it was clear that these alternatives were either not feasible or offered little return for the effort and investment.

RJR's millions of dollars and years sunk into R&D put Targacept in a position of strength and credibility not available to a typical brand new startup. RJR helped Targacept launch itself as a promising spinout with established patents and technologies, world class researchers, and an experienced management team in place. But, just as important as all this nurturing, RJR realized when and how it should step back and set Targacept free.

After a spinout is set free, of course, there is no guarantee of success. As with any new business, it's free to flourish or fail on its own. But with better initial decisions and up-front planning, and with the right kind of nurturing throughout the process, the offspring is better equipped to try to stand and succeed as its own company. That's at least a very promising start.

Employing Spin Control

The bottom line is that, despite all the potential benefits of using spinouts to bring innovation to fruition, these theoretical advantages are far from enough to make a successful spinout. Would-be spinnovators must ask some critical questions up front, before launching into the spinout process:

- **Is the proposed spinout a non-core innovation asset, or is it too close to the core of the company to make sense to spin out as a separate firm?**—In the overwhelming majority of cases, if it's close to the core, a spinout does not make sense and will result in more problems than benefits. Companies need to focus their attention and resources on nurturing and integrating these innovations within the parent company itself.

- **Does the spinout have a sufficiently strong standalone business case, or is it really just a premature idea or ill-formed concept with little hope of a functioning, independent business model?**—If it can't stand on its own, it probably shouldn't be spun out. Nurturing it further internally might not make sense either, especially if it's a non-core innovation. If it is to proceed further, outside partners and investors need to be brought in to help lead it forward to the point where it can be spun out and stand on its own. This helps keep the spinout process from being distracting and detracting for the parent, which can keep a sharper focus on its core.

- **Is the spinout being done for sound strategic reasons or simply to pursue a quick financial boost (for example, to carve off debt and expenses or to get a rapid infusion of cash)?**— Pursuit of short-term, quick-fix financial objectives through a spinout tend to cause long-term complications as the overall logic and structure of the spinout prove dubious and unsustainable over time.

Beyond these critical decision points, one of the most common and most damaging implementation difficulties is when the parent firm simply doesn't know when and how to let go. Too much parenting and too many lingering parent-offspring ties can spoil, smother, or strangle a spinout, even before it really has its own shot at success (see Table 6-2).

Table 6-2 Spin Control

Common Problems	Key Considerations
The Crown Jewels Spinout Spinning out what should not be spun out: spinning out assets too close to the parent's innovation core, carving out a good chunk of the parent's potential future.	Spinnovation should involve assets outside the strategic focus and core competencies of the parent firm. The spunout assets should be non-core; core innovation should not be spun out; the advantages of doing so tend to be illusory or temporary at best.
The One-Legged Stool Spinout A weak case for the spinout as an independent business. A premature idea or a single patent, channel, etc.—not the foundations of a workable and sustainable standalone business model.	The innovation spun out should involve sufficiently complex and incubated assets with real promise to stand and grow as an independent business. An infant idea or single patent or sales channel often does not constitute sufficient foundation for a successful spinout. Integral parts of the parent should not be carved out.
The Piggy-Bank Spinout The spinout decision is driven primarily by pursuit of short-term financial gains or accounting concerns, such as pawning off debt or expenses, sometimes even for core innovation investments.	Long-term strategy, rather than short-term financial exigencies or accounting gimmickry, should be the driving force behind a decision to spin out innovation. When financial considerations are the primary driver, it's a delicate balancing act for all involved. Economic reality often eventually breaks the bank.
The Umbilical-Cord Spinout The spinout isn't truly spun out; it's a partial or faux spinout with too-strong lingering ties to its corporate parent, which effectively makes it a subsidiary at best, and subservient and exploited at worst.	To flourish, the spinout should have its own true decision-making, organizational, and financial independence— real autonomy in terms of both strategy and finances. Minimize complicated and onerous non-market parent-offspring ties. At a minimum, for example, this may require the parent dropping to a minority stake.

A Tale of Online Travel Agents

The overall logic and key questions for planning and implementing a spinout are similar for later-stage (post-commercialization) innovation. The dynamics of these types of spinout decisions are well illustrated in a tale of two online travel agents.

Travel has long been one of the largest and fastest-growing sectors of e-commerce. Through the Internet boom and bust, the online travel business continued to soar. Two of the first and fastest-growing leaders were Expedia, founded by Microsoft, and Travelocity, started by Sabre Holdings (itself an earlier spin-off from American Airlines's parent, AMR Holdings). In one case (Microsoft-Expedia), it made perfect sense to use a spinout to accelerate and enhance further innovation commercialization. In the other case (Sabre-Travelocity), the choice was not so clear and simple, and the process was more complicated.

Microsoft founded Expedia in 1996 as part of its general expansion from software into other online businesses. By 1998, Expedia had quickly grown to become one of the two online travel leaders. Despite Expedia's early success, Microsoft decided that it did not really make sense for it to be in the online travel agent business after all. Microsoft began the process of spinning out Expedia in November 1999, initially selling a 15 percent stake to the public. Soon after, Microsoft sold additional shares, bringing its ownership down to 70 percent. The divestiture was completed in 2001 when Microsoft sold its remaining majority stake for $1.5 billion to USA Interactive, joining it with Interactive's other online travel (Hotels.com, etc.) and retailing operations. As a more clear and core fit with the portfolio of its new parent, Expedia flourished. By 2002, Expedia accounted for almost half of all online gross travel bookings.

Expedia was a tremendously successful later-stage spinout. The online travel agent was an undervalued asset within its parent company, Microsoft. Despite its early success, it simply was not a core concern for Microsoft. There was little connection to Microsoft's other established businesses (operating systems and applications software), which with their huge profit margins and enormous cash flows overshadowed anything Expedia could hope to achieve. Expedia operated an innovative and fast-growing online travel business, but was still burning cash because of its continuing expansion. What to do? Given this entire context, it made perfect strategic sense for Microsoft to spin out Expedia. The spinout created considerable value for all the stakeholders involved.

With Travelocity, however, the story was a bit different. For some time, Sabre Holdings had denied any intent to spin out Travelocity. Unlike Microsoft, after all, Sabre was a leading IT-centered company that handled all sorts of travel-related e-commerce. Sabre executives frequently stressed that Travelocity was part of the core strategy for building the company's future web-based travel businesses. Sabre soon changed its tune, however. The lure of the dot-com spinout frenzy proved to be too great to resist. In March 2000, Sabre spun out Travelocity.com by turning it into a separately traded public company through a reverse merger with Preview Travel. Sabre retained a 70 percent ownership stake.

Travelocity quickly lost its early lead in the online-travel business. An aggressive Expedia became the leader, while Travelocity dropped to less than one-third of online gross bookings. To try to improve its lagging performance, Sabre was now ready to buy back all of Travelocity and, once again, make it a 100 percent–owned subsidiary. In attempting to reverse its spinout, Sabre executives noted that it simply made sense to fully combine Sabre and Travelocity in order to maximize their synergies, especially in core technology and operations.

Travelocity's investors and board balked at Sabre's initial low-ball buyback offer. In a scene too common to spin-ins, Travelocity shareholders filed class-action suits against both parent and spinout, challenging the buyback. Sabre upped its bid from $23 to $28, and a deal finally was struck. Travelocity once again became a wholly owned division of Sabre. Sabre's management reinstalled Travelocity as central to its future. Investment in Travelocity doubled in 2003, even as Sabre significantly cut back its investment in other areas.

The Right Spin

All these spinout examples illustrate the need to consider the specific context—not just the innovation itself, but especially the parent company: its unique strategy, resources, and the like. These cases also illustrate one of our main, overarching points in regard to all the different innovation options—there is no magic bullet, one-size-fits-all solution for all companies in all situations. Just because it might have made great sense for Microsoft to spin out Expedia does not necessarily mean that a Travelocity spinout made sense for Sabre.

The specific context and contingencies—especially the fit with a firm's core innovation—critically matter in deciding whether, when, and how to do a spinout, among all the other innovation options. Like all the other innovations fads and fashions discussed so far, spinouts can liberate and tremendously enhance innovation's value— if they're done right, and for the right reasons. They tend to work best as a supplement, not as a substitute, for core innovation.

7

CONCLUSION
Toward a New Model
for Innovation

"Innovate or die."
—Various

In the wake of the technology boom and bust, the "anything goes" approach to innovation quickly became a tired fad. Successive waves of previously celebrated and much-emulated innovators, both big and small, had stumbled or even failed. Innovation buzzwords formerly spoken with rapt enthusiasm became the subject of deprecating sarcasm. Vague novelty now was severely discounted, not generously rewarded. The deflation of each successive innovation fad and fashion brought disappointment and disillusionment.

Many companies decided to literally cut their losses by shuttering their corporate ventures and VC funds, writing (and shutting) down their acquisitions, ending their alliances, and unwinding their spinouts. They retreated inward, defensively retrenching and refocusing. Much of this introspection was a necessary respite, of course; it gave them a chance to try to regroup and recover from the binge. The overly urgent innovation call-to-arms had quieted, making way for more sober reflection and reconsideration. What, if anything, did we learn?

Despite the myriad missteps and malfunctions, no one seriously doubted that innovation would continue to be a more important and pressing challenge than ever. The New Economy pressures that had driven so many companies to experiment so eagerly had not suddenly disappeared. Although none of the newfangled approaches toward innovation appeared to have worked consistently well in practice, the vast majority of executives and entrepreneurs alike also sensed that a return to the old ways was not a promising, workable answer.

The traditional model for innovation truly was passé. Times had changed. The purveyors of the various "innovation in innovations" were mostly correct in this regard: The old model of innovation no longer worked. In terms of both content (generating new ideas, technologies, and businesses) and structure (the organization necessary to successfully execute these ideas), it fell short. No longer could companies depend entirely on their own "nose-to-the-grindstone" R&D labs and their established internal organizational structures and processes. They no longer were doing the job. An alternative still was sorely needed. This, after all, was precisely why companies big and small had so enthusiastically chased after each successive innovation fad and fashion as it had emerged. The question was: Where do we go from here?

Amidst all the wreckage and reassessment, a new model for profitable and sustainable innovation began to more clearly emerge. By grappling with their own particular post-bubble challenges, many companies began the process of discovering and implementing, shaping and refining, this new approach. Few explicitly articulated the new design, however. This is one of our key objectives in concluding our broad-ranging discussion of various innovations in innovation.

Core Complexity

The emerging model for innovation is both simpler at its core, and yet overall considerably more complex than any of its predecessors. First, the new paradigm is simpler because of its renewed emphasis on the central, foundational importance of core innovation. There was a sense among many, if not agreement among all, that organizations should no longer bet their future on juggling dozens of diverse, peripheral, and experimental ventures in the hope that somehow, somewhere, one of these marginal "real options" would strike "in the money" big time. Instead, committed and integrated innovation with *focus* and *fit* is the real challenge, and the real source of rich rewards.

Overall, however, the emerging innovation paradigm is much more complex than the old traditional, inward-focused, internal R&D approach. It's also more complex than any single one of the largely transactional remedies promised by each of the individual innovation fads and fashions. In sum, the new model is more complex because it increasingly requires organizations to focus on generating and nourishing core innovation, even while simultaneously maintaining a more active balance of innovation sourcing and peripheral experimentation from both inside and outside. It therefore requires deft mastery of more numerous and varied sets of tools. These tools include, in their proper place and perspective, not just one, but *all* the innovation tactics we have discussed: venturing, licensing, alliances, acquisitions, and spinouts. The new model therefore is not a simple quick fix. Instead, it's a more complicated and dynamic mix. But it's a mix that also is more rational, effective, and sustainable.

Many of the old innovation skills and goals remain essential. Without a strong internal R&D culture and without home-grown innovation, for example, there is little grounding and coherent direction for a firm's overall innovation strategy. An innovation strategy with a strong internal core is the best source of a sustainable competitive advantage. Just as important, it's the base and leverage with which to effectively and profitably exploit even outsourced innovations in a superior fashion.

The new model for innovation requires more than a flourishing organic innovation culture, however. It also requires the complementary addition of more open elements of culture, new sets of skills, and different types of objectives. It requires a strategy and organization that can foster the power and pride of "Invented Here," even as it can rapidly identify and effectively assimilate Not Invented Here (NIH). This is a very different and challenging sort of balance, but it's far from an impossible task. This is, in fact, the new essence and the principal goal of the emerging model of innovation.

Lessons Learned: Rediscovering the Core

One key lesson learned from the aftermath of all the innovation fads and fashions was that core innovation must be the primary investment. What all the innovation fads and fashions had in common was that, in both presentation and execution, they tended to ignore, neglect, or distract (and therefore ultimately detract) from core innovation. They ventured further and further from the real strategies and real businesses that begged for innovation the most, the massive and looming problems and challenges that really needed novel ideas, new technologies, and fresh approaches. Disconnected from their companies' cores, little guide or grounding existed for these innovation experiments. There were few strategies, mostly just tactics; it was novelty for novelty's sake. As a result, many of these adventures were set up to fail from the beginning, not given a head-start boost as promised.

In contrast, at the center of the new model for innovation is a renewed appreciation for, and focus on, core innovation. Profitable and sustainable innovation is not about wanton novelty at the periphery. It's not about abandoning a firm's core R&D, organization, channels, and customers because they're just too "old" and "tired." In extreme but extraordinarily rare cases (such as the rapid, impending decline or destruction of an entire technology, company, or industry), abruptly abandoning the old might make sense. But this is extraordinarily uncommon, and even in these cases, it's rarely a completely sudden event with no opportunity to adjust. A firm's innovation core is still most often the guiding force by which to plan and execute such a transformation. Even with the need for radical change, transforming the old core—not completely abandoning it—usually is a superior value-creating bet, one with much better odds.

The CEO of bakery-café casual chain Au Bon Pain managed to pull off such a rare transformation when he jettisoned the flagging core brand, refocused on a newer and more upscale concept, and rebirthed the entire company as Panera Bread. Au Bon Pain had acquired the Panera Bread concept with its purchase of the small St. Louis Bread Co. chain. By 1999, Panera had grown to almost 200 stores. With slowing sales and operational difficulties at the core Au Bon Pain franchise, going forward, the new concept looked to be the more attractive option. The Au Bon Pain name and chain were sold off and Panera Bread was born.

Even in this very uncommon and relatively radical case, the successful innovation transformation was not a wholesale leap from the essence of the original business. The focus was still casual dining, centered around bread, baked goods, sandwiches, and coffee. Au Bon Pain initially used an acquisition to infuse new concepts to the chain. It developed and incubated them further internally over a period of five years. Only then did it use the entire initiative as a launch pad to vault to a new (although still closely related) innovation core. This transformation also was made much more plausible by the fact that it was a relatively small and simple company.

A related lesson from the innovation boom and bust is that the dire, urgent warnings about the need for rapid and radical innovation at all costs most often proved unwarranted. Despite all the breathless excitement about the need to innovate or die, the fact remains that most established businesses were not displaced and replaced by agile and tech-savvy upstarts. Established retailers and manufacturers, from financial service companies to health-care providers, were not upended and overtaken by technology. More often than not, in fact, the established leaders became the survivors or "thrivors." The success of innovative thrivors Dell, Wal-Mart, and Southwest Airlines long predated the technology bubble, for example, yet each company used the power of the Internet to leverage their core marketing and operational capabilities toward even greater industry domination. They used their existing core innovation as a base and as leverage with which to more quickly and fully exploit the potential of the Internet in order to enhance their already formidable advantages.

These are three of the most successful cases, but they're not entirely exceptional by any means. The fact remains that most successful, established companies proceeded to adopt and adapt major innovations, whether through organic development or external acquisition, throughout the technology ferment. It was never a completely smooth process, but neither was it an impossible struggle, contrary to much of the advice and many of the prescriptions at the time. Those established firms that failed or lagged tended to be slow casualties of longer-term trends, especially internal dysfunctions such as deteriorating core innovation. They rarely were blindsided victims of some sudden technological revolution.

The implication of these dynamics is that, for the vast majority of contexts and decisions, core innovation is what powers companies forward and, consequently, what must be their continued emphasis, even as the latest and greatest new ideas and technologies take flight. An established company cannot ignore its legacy and hope for innovation salvation from some wild and far-flung venturing experiment, an expensive hot bet on an early stage, R&D-driven, long-shot acquisition, or a clever but convoluted new-tech spinout. Even when such ventures are successful in their own right, decay at the core might continue or even accelerate. Even successful off-line experiments rarely are sufficient to offset the loss of the chance for renewal in a firm's core, and the consequent likely destruction of enormous amounts of value.

Using New Tools to Power the Core

To power the core, *all* the new approaches to innovation we have explored in the previous chapters are increasingly critical for innovation success. They work best to infuse, not replace, the core. To this end, what has powerfully propelled most of the successful innovators forward through the innovation boom and bust and beyond has *not* been a return to their old ways. They have not retrenched to a single-minded focus on internal R&D and "sticking to their knitting." Nor have these companies jettisoned their core to aimlessly chase after some even more newfangled innovation experiment. In fact, in each case, refocusing on their cores has served as the fundamental guide and indispensable anchor for their renewed innovation strategies. With such strong grounding, they've then been able to successfully experiment—both inside and outside their organizations—to create, capture, and exploit the innovation they need, from whatever the source.

The examples range from formerly tarnished names such as McDonald's and Procter & Gamble, companies that stumbled but managed to regain much of their former glow, to younger brand-name exemplars such as Starbucks, companies that grew restless during innovation mania but that regained their focus. The examples also include entrepreneurial firms that are dominant in their own market space, firms like Replacements Limited and its transformation to Replacements.com.

In each of the earlier chapters, we dedicate considerable discussion to the innovation challenges of myriad cutting-edge, high-tech companies. The following examples take the cutting-edge technology down a level. However, the lessons about the importance of core innovation are just as applicable to hi-tech and low-tech companies alike.

Leveraging the Core: Little Things Mean a Lot

The simple and familiar example of McDonald's shows the profound importance, and the power and leverage, of core innovation. By 2002, McDonald's corporate venturing with its diverse Chipotle, Donatos, and Boston Market chains had contributed relatively little to its revenues and profits—in fact, mostly big losses—during the previous few years. Fast-food price wars involving the core McDonald's franchise also had taken their toll. Cheaper burgers were only fattening more and more waistlines, not the company's bottom line.

In December 2002, in the wake of several disappointing quarters, McDonald's CEO stepped down. A *Wall Street Journal* story summed up the stark situation that any new management team would confront: "McDonald's Corp. gave investors more heartburn, warning that the company expects to report its first quarterly loss since going public 37 years ago." McDonald's stock slid to a new multiyear low, slashing billions from its market capitalization. Retired former international chief Jim Cantalupo returned to McDonald's as the new CEO to tackle what undoubtedly would be a long and tough job ahead.

Only a year later, however, the headlines were far different and McDonald's stock surged. It posted record cash flow for 2003 and a big year-end boost in sales and profits. What radical shift helped produce such phenomenal results? A key part of the quick turnaround was simply the introduction of new core product offerings. Some products were more "radically" innovative than others, but together they all helped tip the company's momentum in the right direction. McGriddles, for example, upgraded and updated the venerable Egg McMuffin in a unique, convenient, and satisfying (if not all that healthy) sweet pancake-sandwiched breakfast meal. At the same time, the chain's healthier-option premium meal salads appealed to a different crowd, yet without the stigma of its earlier infamous offerings like the much maligned "seaweed" burger, the McLean Deluxe.

McDonald's new management team emphasized that igniting a turnaround involved more than McGriddles and salads. But both were critically symbolic of a larger refocusing on core innovation in McDonald's main lines of business. Both offerings promised fast, consistent, and satisfying food. They offered taste, convenience, and value. People who hadn't visited McDonald's in a while started to come back and visit more often.

Kids of all ages could indulge in new tastes like McGriddles, even while leaner white-meat McNuggets and healthier Happy Meals also appeared on the menu. Perhaps more importantly, customers who had abandoned McDonald's convenience and consistency in pursuit of lighter tastes now could grab a quick, quality meal salad. The healthier, updated salad offerings were a big hit among athletes at the Summer 2004 Athens Olympics, for example, a key part of McDonald's ongoing global marketing and sponsorship efforts. Consistent with these efforts, the company nixed its Super Size menu option as a matter of policy in mid 2004, just prior to the wide release of the obesity shock-umentary *Super Size Me*. With fortuitous timing, this stream of seemingly small but collectively significant shifts helped blunt an imminent tobacco-style attack on fast food that was clearly targeted at McDonald's.

Even so, McDonald's did not abandon its classic burgers and fries by any means. Instead, it revamped and renewed its core mix of offerings to powerful effect. The average salad-buyer meal tab, for example, totaled nearly double that of the more typical burgers-and-fries crowd.

Protracted fast-food price wars were out; core innovation was back in. With more than 30,000 outlets worldwide and greater than $40 billion in annual system-wide revenues, McDonald's 10 percent year-over-year boost in fourth-quarter 2003 sales was not an insignificant event. Given the enormous leverage of McDonald's core business, little things clearly mean a lot.

At the same time, McDonald's announced the sale or closing of many of the experimental, non-core brands and joint ventures, including Donatos Pizza and Fazoli's. Just a couple years earlier, much of McDonald's hopes centered on the promise of new growth with these supposedly more updated and upscale concept ventures. In contrast to these drawn-out, cash-draining experiments, however, the sudden revival of McDonald's core business created enormous value in a relative flash. The stock more than doubled from its low.

Under the umbrella of McDonald's Ventures, however, the company did retain the Chipotle Mexican Grill chain and the U.S. Boston Market franchise. Few questioned the company's retaining these ventures, at least experimentally. Henceforth, they would be developed and funded largely of their own accord. With a new strategy, McDonald's put corporate venturing more in its proper place and perspective: as an experiment and as a learning tool, and possibly as a longer-term bet, but not to the neglect of core innovation. The company renewed its focus and righted the balance between core innovation and venturing.

Unfortunately, tragic events struck McDonald's in 2004. Yet even these terrible events helped further illustrate the durable and profitable power of core innovation. With his fresh new strategy still very much a work in progress, Jim Cantalupo suddenly died of a heart attack in April. Then, just two weeks later, Cantalupo's relatively youthful 43-year old successor, Charlie Bell, received grim news. Bell told the board and the world that he would be fighting a serious battle with cancer. In another short couple of weeks, Bell had surgery and began a rigorous round of chemotherapy.

Despite the tremendous challenges that these events presented in rapid-fire succession—the sort of turmoil that could easily send a company reeling—under Bell's leadership, McDonald's continued to power forward with its renewal. Second-quarter 2004 sales increased 10 percent, and profits leapt 25 percent. Margins grew to nearly 20 percent, the highest in a decade. Overall, for the first six months of 2004, net income was up 33 percent compared to the same year-earlier period.

McDonald's clearly still faced serious challenges, both in terms of continuing to refine and execute its new strategy and in terms of ongoing uncertainty about its leadership. With little doubt, however, these early results provided a substantial down payment on its renewed investments in core innovation—a performance all the more remarkable in the face of such sudden adversity and uncertainty.

Fueling the Core: Innovating Beyond the Obvious

Core innovation often goes far beyond tweaking existing products or even reinvigorating entire product categories. Sometimes, it doesn't involve the core product directly much at all. Nonetheless, the leveraged power of core innovation can take even relatively minor new ideas and technologies and turn them into substantial gains; little things mean a lot. This dynamic can be seen in a technology-related example from Starbucks that has little to do with coffee directly, but much to do with enhancing the delivery of "the coffee experience."

Starbucks was one of the more fantastic innovation success stories of the 1990s. Even as per-capita coffee consumption plummeted by 50 percent during the previous three decades, Starbucks launched and thrived. It offered the relatively unique experience of made-to-order, ready-to-drink, barista-manned espresso coffee outlets that were oddly positioned somewhere between a McDonald's and an authentic European café. It let customers buy into the espresso experience. It let them feel special to splurge on an affordable luxury and get their caffeine and sugar fixes at the same time. Having a slightly addictive product didn't hurt either.

Even Starbucks got distracted and caught up in Internet fever, however. During the height of froth over the web, company founder Howard Schultz uttered his instantly infamous line that Starbucks would henceforth be an Internet company. More than a few people were scratching their heads trying to figure out what that meant. In 1999, Schultz explained his goal of setting up a separate Internet venture division to push the Starbucks brand and experience into e-tailing and other forms of online communing and commerce. Most observers thought it was fortuitous that Starbucks never got very far with the idea before the bottom fell out of the dot-com craze. Starbucks quietly shelved the idea and refocused on delivering the coffee experience.

Starbucks did have a future in e-commerce, only of a different sort. In late 2001, the chain introduced the Starbucks Card, a stored-value payment card. What do coffee and stored-value cards have in common? On the surface, not much. But the cards made it easier, faster, and cheaper to get one's urgent caffeine fix at the corner Starbucks café. Customers could buy stored-value Starbucks Cards and then pay for their usual cup with a simple swipe. No fumbling for change, and the cards could easily be refreshed online at Starbucks's web site. Later, Starbucks co-branded credit cards were introduced, with rapidly earned rewards in the form of espressos and lattés.

Starbucks was a habit. The cards made the habit even more convenient to indulge. Same-store sales perked up significantly. Now Chairman Howard Schultz and CEO Orin Smith both noted that the Starbucks Cards were one of the most significant and successful Starbucks innovations since the Frappuccino was introduced with great success in the mid 1990s. Another core innovation, the Frappuccino initially garnered little enthusiasm among Starbucks leadership, but within a few years, it became a billion-dollar business in its own right.

A co-developed, stored-value payment card as a core innovation for a coffee chain? It's a gimmick that would not have worked nearly as well for most types of retailers or food-service establishments.

Few chains have so many locations and with such a loyal base of customers visiting so regularly and frequently. The cards made loyalists visit and buy all the more. It was a perfect fit for Starbucks that honed their focus on delivering "the coffee experience." Although Starbucks Cards were a seemingly tangential innovation to the company's main product and service offerings, they nonetheless significantly bolstered Starbucks's coffee business. They fueled the core.

Transforming the Core: Internalizing Radical Innovation

At very rare but critical times, the challenges of innovation justify (or even require) a more radical and transformative approach. The aforementioned case of Panera Bread is one such example. The rapid evolution of Replacements Limited to Replacements.com provides another good illustration of a radical core transformation, and of how it can strongly invigorate an already powerful business model.

Replacements Limited had been in business for 15 years before e-commerce really emerged as a channel. The company already had built a lucrative $50 million-plus annual business by making itself the leading, go-to source for replacement china, crystal, silverware, and similar housewares. Originally, it seemed a bit of a quirky business idea; that the concept raised some eyebrows when founder and CEO Bob Page first floated it. The idea was an outgrowth of his flea-market hobby, after all: collecting china and crystal, collectibles, and the like. Page was denied small-business loans by state officials who told him the strange concept "would never work."

Quirky or not, more than a few people were willing to pay for the value Replacements Limited provided. Customers could easily and quickly replace a lost or broken item in their heirloom or wedding set of china or crystal, for example, rather than having to buy a whole new set for thousands more. Relieved and gratified patrons were willing to pay good margins for such service and product. It was a fantastic win-win value proposition for both customers and Replacements Limited. Replacements so thoroughly dominated its market by the late 1990s that the next largest competitor was only about 1 percent its size. Replacements Limited had built a nationwide network of suppliers and had amassed an unrivaled inventory of millions of patterns and items.

With the advent of the Internet, however, e-commerce offered a host of challenges. The web directly presented technology and channel challenges for a firm that had been doing business primarily by phone and mail, with just one retail outlet for more than 15 years. The web also presented some unprecedented competition, especially one called eBay. Although it was not a direct competitor, eBay was probably the biggest threat that Replacements Limited had ever faced. Customers might simply tap into eBay's limitless virtual inventory of virtually everything and anything to try to find and acquire replacement items, and therefore bypass Replacements Limited altogether. By 1998, Replacements Limited had to decide whether to jump on board the dot-com bandwagon: Should it create a new Internet venture division, or should it form a new dot-com spinout as so many other companies were doing?

Replacements chose neither path. Instead, CEO Bob Page decided to transform the entire core of the enterprise. Replacements Limited began a methodical but rapid transition to become Replacements.com. They eschewed high-priced IT consultants who were hawking their latest-and-greatest, bells-and-whistles web technology. Instead, for a fraction of the price, Replacements developed and implemented its far-reaching adaptation to e-commerce primarily with its own in-house expertise, supplemented from outside as necessary. Its developers focused on quickly creating basic Internet functionality, including fast-to-load and easy-to-use web pages. The completed system gave customers access not only to full pricing and product information, but also offered transparent real-time access to Replacements's own inventory databases.

The process had its challenges. By committing wholesale to the initiative, however, Replacements's essential transformation was achieved in less than a year and for less than $1 million. Replacements Limited quickly and effectively transformed into Replacements.com, doing the majority of its business on the web. Within a few years, sales increased nearly 50 percent, even as its Internet adaptations significantly lowered both operating and marketing costs. Privately held Replacements.com not only survived the dot-com downturn, but positively thrived throughout the turmoil.

By 2002, *Internet Retailer* named Replacements.com a leader in e-commerce, along with other much larger colleagues, such as Amazon.com and eBay. For Replacements Limited, taking its old-fashioned business model and venturing online was not a peripheral experiment. Instead, Replacements Limited successfully identified and tackled the challenge as one requiring the methodical yet rapid transformation of the entire firm.

Core Innovation ≠ Internal R&D

It's critically important to note that, in emphasizing the centrality of core innovation as a fundamental guiding principle, we emphatically are not endorsing a nostalgic return to the old internal R&D myopia or a simple, inward-focused "stick to the knitting" approach. Internal R&D and new business development are vital, foundational ingredients in the innovation mix. However, core innovation can come from anywhere, from either inside or outside the organization. Keeping it all inside, organic R&D alone is not the answer, and it is certainly not our recommendation. The cases we discuss in each chapter illustrate this well:

- RF Micro Devices (see Chapter 3) could not have long existed, much less flourished, without first striking a manufacturing alliance with, and then later in-licensing key technology from, TRW. Despite years of effort and development of their own technology and patent portfolio, RF Micro Devices's internal R&D was simply not sufficient to bring their innovation to fruition. TRW's gallium arsenide semiconductor technology was a critically necessary key to unlock RF Micro Devices's latent value, making the license worth even the rich price of one-third of the company. Later, as the wireless semiconductor industry continued to evolve, RF Micro Devices began to ink both R&D M&A deals and new R&D and manufacturing alliances to try to gain expertise and capabilities in silicon chips and chipsets, areas quite a bit beyond their core competencies in gallium arsenide, even as the company continued to invest more in its own internal R&D efforts. Almost from RF Micro Devices's inception, core innovation never implied simply toiling away at its own narrowly focused internal R&D.

- Biopharmaceutical startup Trimeris (see Chapter 4) needed more than just the cash and marketing resources that a licensing deal with a Big Pharma partner might provide. It also just as critically needed a partner to help it work out the complicated and expensive manufacturing and delivery processes for its novel compounds to treat drug-resistant HIV. In turn, Roche's alliance with Trimeris helped it more fully fill out its own portfolio of AIDS drugs, including its own internally developed compounds. In this case, internal research, development, and commercialization was not the solution for either company; a focused and tightly managed innovation partnership was. Their integral strategic alliance further powered core innovation for both firms.

- Cisco Systems (see Chapter 5) never could have been built into such a dominating force in its core networking business solely on the merits of its own internal R&D. Exploratory alliances often paved the way for the company's subsequent stream of innovation by acquisition. It's certainly true that some of the acquisitions were overpriced and underperformed (especially the later ones), and some even outright failed. And it's also true that, in the wake of the technology bust, Cisco abruptly halted its M&A strategy and decided to refocus more on internal R&D. Nonetheless, a good portion of Cisco's earlier M&A approach was appropriate and effective given the technology and industry dynamics that prevailed throughout much of the 1990s. Aggressive innovation by acquisition worked well in the early and mid-1990s, even if it was less successful during the peak of the M&A binge that followed. As circumstances changed, Cisco rebalanced its portfolio of innovation sourcing and modes; it reconsidered and de-emphasized R&D by M&A, even as it nonetheless maintained acquisition as a very real option in its overall arsenal. When the smoke of the technology bust cleared, Cisco rekindled its R&D by M&A strategy, but with fewer pricey deals and many more bargains in the mix.

- A need to focus on creating value through core innovation sometimes also suggests the need to spin out *non-core* innovation, regardless of (or perhaps precisely because of) how great its potential value might be. Microsoft and R.J. Reynolds (see Chapter 6) couldn't internally develop Expedia and Targacept, respectively, if they wanted to let these innovations fully bloom. Both sought to focus more on their own core businesses. Consequently, online travel leader Expedia.com and biopharmaceutical startup Targacept probably never would have had the chance to flourish as they did unless and until they were spun out and set loose from their corporate parents. In the process of divestiture, what were peripheral innovations for Microsoft and R.J. Reynolds became compelling core innovations for the newly freed and focused spinouts themselves.

In each of these cases, the emphasis is on core innovation, but the mechanisms for achieving the ends are complex and eclectic. A nostalgic return to internal R&D, therefore, is clearly not the answer and is certainly not our suggestion.

Instead, what we're recommending is a more open-minded but well-grounded approach to innovation: considering and using all the external, transactional options that are available as necessary and appropriate, yet with a strong internal R&D and new business development foundation. That is, companies need to develop the knowledge and skills to quickly identify and effectively implement opportunities for venturing, licensing, alliances, acquisitions, and spinouts. At the center of it all, however, they must build and nourish the core resources and capabilities that provide both strategic direction and competitive advantage for the entire constellation of innovation sources and modes they bring together. Core innovation, from whatever the source, must have focus and fit. It needs to be central and integrated, not peripheral and off-line. The core is the nexus that guides and enhances value creation and value capture for what otherwise would be an overly complex yet increasingly hollow holding company or venture capital fund.

The New Model ≠ Open Market Innovation

It's also important to emphasize that, in advocating proactive consideration and incorporation of external sources of innovation, neither are we advising undue reliance or too-narrow focus on Not Invented Here (NIH). Just as it's not all about internal R&D, nor does the emerging model revolve around loose concepts such as open-market innovation (i.e., better and faster R&D deal making). It's not centered around freeform and opportunistic external sourcing of innovation. As we discussed earlier in regard to licensing and acquisition, for example, there's no such thing as a free lunch. You tend to get what you pay for or, in many cases, you simply tend to pay too much.

Open-market innovation comes with its own price and risks. If you want ready-to-go innovation, you'd better have a thick checkbook. After you finish paying the purchase price, there might be little chance left of ever earning a decent return on your substantial up-front investment. If you're willing to take on a bit more of the risk of buying early stage innovation in exchange for a lower price, you'd better be prepared for unexpected setbacks and potentially heavy further development costs. The bottom line is that the only way to consistently earn superior profits from externally sourced innovations is to have some idiosyncratic advantage, especially a strong position in your own distinctive innovation core, that enables you to recognize, internalize, and commercialize these external ideas, technologies, and products in a way that no one else in the market could do nearly as well. That's how consistent, superior profitability is created and sustained.

Fueling Core Innovation from Inside and Outside

The recent experience of Procter & Gamble provides a clear example of the trend toward a more complex, but simultaneously more focused and better grounded, new model for innovation. By the late 1990s, Procter & Gamble hungered for growth and renewal. Judgments from inside and outside the company agreed that something needed to be done. Sales stalled. New product introductions were sparse and slow.

Procter & Gamble had fallen victim to what had been for decades a strong and effective internal R&D culture that had simply gone stale over time. It now was perceived as a slothful, conservative, over-engineering, and inward-focused organization. It had become a dated exemplar of the formerly well-honed, but now sputtering, model of internal R&D and organic new business development. A new management team under the leadership of CEO Durk Jager began implementing a broad-ranging global restructuring designed to power more innovation to market faster and more broadly. Simultaneously, like so many of its blue-chip colleagues, Procter & Gamble embarked on numerous experiments in corporate venturing: skunkworks, venture capital, Internet incubators, and more.

Unfortunately, all this radical action did not alleviate concerns about Procter & Gamble from either inside or outside the organization. Indeed, many soon worried that the proposed cure might be worse than the disease. The wrenching restructuring caused considerable disruption and discord within Procter & Gamble's vital country and brand units, which had long featured some of the best consumer goods expertise in the world. Much of Procter & Gamble's talent departed. Meanwhile, after only a couple years in progress, it seemed clear that Procter & Gamble's many novel corporate-venturing initiatives were doing relatively little to revive Procter & Gamble's larger global prospects.

Jager announced disappointing results in early March 2000. The resulting massive drop in Procter & Gamble's decidedly blue-chip stock gave a preview of the imminent technology-led market crash yet to come. Procter & Gamble's shares fell by almost one-third in one day. Such a plunge would have been big news even for a speculative technology stock. The one-day drop was especially shocking for a supposedly stable and established company like Procter & Gamble.

In mid 2000, Procter & Gamble veteran A.G. Lafley took over as the new CEO and immediately set out to stabilize a restive organization. He did not abandon all of Jager's initiatives and ideas, but rather sought to better balance and clarify Procter & Gamble's innovation strategy. It was henceforth to be a strategy clearly centered on core innovation. But it was far from a nostalgic return to Procter & Gamble's old days and old ways. In fact, Lafley demanded that Procter & Gamble's innovators more aggressively seek core innovation wherever they could find it, both inside and outside:

> The key element of P&Gs growth strategy can most simply be described as growth from the core. We are building on P&G's core foundation of categories and brands, customers and countries, capabilities and competencies to deliver long-term, sustainable growth. . . .

> We're multiplying this capability by collaborating
> more extensively with external innovation partners.
> The vision is that 50 percent of all P&G discovery
> and invention will come from outside the Company.

The experience of Procter & Gamble's Crest brand shows how the new model came together in practice. The Crest Whitestrips tooth-whitening product had been developed internally and was introduced in late 2000. Also in 2000, the Crest Spinbrush line of low-cost battery-powered toothbrushes was acquired from Dr. John's Spinbrush, the fast-growing category pioneer and leader. Crest Whitestrips quickly grew to more than $300 million in sales in a strong new subcategory with even greater future expansion and extension potential. Meanwhile, the Crest Spinbrush line closely followed, soon doubling its post-acquisition sales to more than $200 million, also in a new subcategory with solid further potential for development.

Both innovations helped rejuvenate a seriously flagging core Procter & Gamble brand and category. Colgate, with a powerful core innovation of its own in the antibacterial Total line of tooth-pastes, had in the previous few years seized the lead from Crest and left it listless and wanting. Crest Whitestrips and Crest Spinbrush—one born and developed inside the company and one bought and integrated from the outside—both helped boost Procter & Gamble's core innovation in oral care and its core Crest brand. These successes were followed by other related innovations that boosted the entire brand and overall category.

As Procter & Gamble posted such solid gains, the company regained much of its luster. Its recovery was powered by innovations far beyond oral care—from Olay Daily Facials to Febreze fabric refreshener to Mr. Clean Magic Eraser and the Swiffer line of cleaning products. These other new additions also came from both inside and outside. Procter & Gamble's Prilosec OTC antacid product was the result of an alliance and licensing deal with European-based pharmaceutical company AstraZeneca, for example. The venture tapped into Procter & Gamble's considerable consumer packaged goods resources and capabilities to take the former leading prescription anti-acid drug to a much broader, non-prescription customer base. Prilosec OTC's introduction in late 2003 was a notable success, reinforcing Procter & Gamble's reputation as the preferred partner for taking former prescription-only drugs to the larger over-the-counter (OTC) mass market.

With a series of solid base hits, Procter & Gamble shares soon nearly doubled from their 2000 lows. It was fitting that, in the wake of the technology and market bust, venerable old Procter & Gamble would chart a new path and begin to try to better outline and implement its own version of the emerging new model for innovation. Procter & Gamble chose to expand its portfolio of innovation sources and modes, even as it renewed the purpose and refocused the direction of its core innovation strategy.

Importance of Portfolio and Process

The emerging new model for innovation increasingly is about building and balancing a dynamic portfolio of innovation options—venturing, licensing, alliances, acquisitions, and spinouts—but all nourishing and continually renewing a vibrant core base. Organizations must look "outside" and be able to recognize and embrace Not Invented Here (NIH) when necessary. They need to get more comfortable and facile with externally focused, transactional approaches to R&D. At the same time, it's not all about ungrounded, deal-driven open-market innovation. The panoply of choices needs to be guided by core strategic concerns of focus and fit, and integrated with and leveraged by the firm's own solid innovation foundation. At the nexus of the entire dynamic portfolio is a thriving, bustling innovation core (see Figure 7-1).

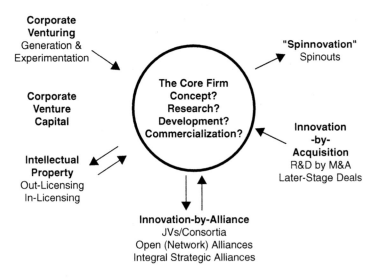

Figure 7-1 Emerging new model for innovation.

Choosing and using each of the individual innovation options, as well as building and balancing the entire portfolio, is part of an ongoing process. Each individual option, as well as the entire portfolio, cannot be effectively pursued as static, one-time, adhoc investments. In a now common sort of progression, for example, investment in a startup might, in the future, transform into an alliance or in-licensing deal, possibly later become an acquisition, then perhaps be followed by out-licensing or spinout of excess, non-core innovation that's been acquired. Evaluating and implementing each approach therefore demands ongoing consideration of the specific objectives, resources, and context. Companies must consider and plan for the evolution of different choices, and of the entire portfolio. They must be prepared to change their tactics and strategies as circumstances dictate. Managing this complexity and dynamism is undeniably challenging, but this juggling act is key to surviving and thriving. It's how even established firms can keep up with—or, better yet, even stay ahead of—the innovation curve.

Innovation Redeemed and Revitalized

So, where does this journey through the ups and downs of various innovation fads and fashions finally leave us? Clearly, there is no simple, quick, and universal solution to fuel innovation all the way from conception to commercialization, especially not for all organizations in all situations. In this sense, all the innovation fads and fashions overpromised and underdelivered. Often, they were recommended and applied at the wrong time, or for the wrong reasons, organizations, or situations. They were promoted and adopted with little attention or concern for the critical nuances of their implementation and evolution.

In contrast, we offer no pretense that this is a "recipe" book. Innovation cannot be reduced to simple templates or standard prescriptions. We do, however, believe that all the approaches to innovation present inherent tensions and conflicts, problems and pitfalls, caveats and conditions that beg to be heeded. As we have explored throughout this book, the "how" of innovation matters as much as the "what" in determining innovation success and failure. Innovation initiatives need to be designed up front to have the best chances of success, not set up to fail.

In each chapter, therefore, we provide an overview and summary of key lessons learned in regard to each particular innovation tool or tactic: When is this or that approach a good bet or a worse bet? What are the pitfalls to watch out for and avoid? What are the key details to consider and plan for, thinking ahead? What are the better and worse approaches toward maneuvering and managing the critical details of implementation? In addition to these specific issues, there also are a few more general conclusions that can be drawn from our larger exploration of the innovation landscape.

Certainly, the experiences of the past few years leave one a bit more skeptical, but perhaps also more hopeful. The hope flows from at least two sources. First, these experiments and experiences ultimately have led to a renewed and more coherent focus on core value creation. Second, each of the innovation fads and fashions, in their own way, had much to offer as part of building a more diverse and dynamic portfolio of innovation options and choices. Each idea brought essential new value, a vitally useful new tool and tactic, to the innovation workshop, even if many kinks had to be worked out in practice.

Building from a solid foundation of core innovation, in fact, all these tools and tactics offer more realistic and effective solutions to the most critical innovation challenges of companies big and small alike. They offer real hope to large and established organizations seeking new ways to create and capture value without abandoning their own unique strengths and legacies. They likewise offer new approaches by which young, entrepreneurial startups can minimize their weaknesses and leverage their own novel resources and capabilities in order to grow and prosper.

In an increasingly complicated, fast-moving, and technology-driven global economy, deft mastery of these varied approaches will only grow more important. This means being able to craft and balance more complex portfolios, and manage evolving processes, in which any or all of these innovation tools and tactics might play important roles. The task is made even more complex by the fact that innovation increasingly crosses borders of all kinds, taking on new international dimensions and involving, what is for many organizations, still relatively unfamiliar global territory. Ideas and talent are everywhere. This fact will drive everything from increased cross-border in-licensing and out-licensing, to increased corporate venture capital investments in (and from) places like China and India, to more international alliances and acquisitions. It's a brave new world of more diverse and dynamic innovation taking shape.

The emerging new model we've described is not a simple panacea. Nor is it some fantastically novel, supposedly breakthrough scheme (read: fad or fashion). But it is a more realistic, effective, and sustainable approach. And it is surely the future of innovation.

Endnotes

Chapter 1

1. For example, Michael Schrage and Matthew Boyle. "Getting beyond the innovation fetish." *Fortune*. November 13, 2000.

2. A great overview of the entire saga is *Smartest Guys in the Room: The Amazing Rise and Scandalous Fall of Enron* by Bethany McLean and Peter Elkind (2003).

3. "Business: Hatching a new plan." *The Economist*. August 12, 2000.

Chapter 2

1. Corporate venturing is not synonymous with corporate innovation in general, or with more specific but traditional and

integrated functions such as new business development. In theory and practice, corporate venturing specifically refers to the founding and funding of distinct internal structures and processes, different from those of the established core organization, yet ultimately still part of the parent firm.

2. For example, Gary Hamel. "Bringing Silicon Valley Inside." *Harvard Business Review*. September 1999; Heidi Mason and Tim Rohner. *The Venture Imperative*. 2002; Clayton Christensen. *The Innovator's Dilemma*. 1997.

3. In fact, corporate venture capital has historically tended to follow a boom-and-bust wave that tracks the rise and fall of independent venture capital funds. A good historical overview of corporate venture capital is by Paul A. Gompers, "Corporations and the financing of innovation: The corporate venturing experience." *Economic Review—Federal Reserve Bank of Atlanta*. Fourth Quarter 2002.

4. Brent Schendler. "How the chips were won." *Business 2.0*, January/February 2004.

5. In addition to our own analyses, other studies are also consistent with this finding. For example, Paul A. Gompers. "Corporations and the financing of innovation: The corporate venturing experience." *Economic Review—Federal Reserve Bank of Atlanta*. Fourth Quarter 2002.

Chapter 3

1. For example, Dyan Machan. "An Edison for a new age?" *Forbes*. May 17, 1999; Kevin G. Rivette and David Kline. *Rembrandts in the Attic: Unlocking the Hidden Value of Patents*. 2000.

2. For example, Thomas A. Stewart. *Intellectual Capital: The New Wealth of Organizations*. 1998.

3. "It was my idea." *The Economist*. August 15, 1998.

4. Holman W. Jenkins, Jr. "Busting the intellectual property bubble." *The Wall Street Journal*. March 29, 2000.

5. Eric von Hippel. *The Sources of Innovation*. 1997–1998.

6. Microsoft generated enormous revenues from *product* licensing but not from IP licensing. A critical distinction exists between product licensing (finished products) and the licensing of "unfinished" IP (the building blocks of innovation). Product licensing is more of a manufacturing and/or distribution concern, not a core R&D issue.

7. John Carey. "The genome gold rush: Who will be the first to hit pay dirt?" *Business Week*. June 12, 2000.

8. Declan Butler. "Drive for patent-free innovation gathers pace." *Nature*. July 10, 2003.

Chapter 4

1. For example, Yves Doz and Gary Hamel. *The Alliance Advantage*. 1998.

2. For example, James F. Moore. *The Death of Competition*. 1997; Adam M. Brandenburger and Barry J. Nalebuff. *Co-opetition*. 1997, and "The Right Game: Use Game Theory to Shape Strategy." *Harvard Business Review*. July 1995; Morten T. Hansen, Henry W. Chesbrough, Nitin Nohria, and Donald Sull. "Networked Incubators: Hothouses of the New Economy." *Harvard Business Review*. September 2000.

3. Leslie Cauley. "Losses in Space—Iridium's Downfall." *The Wall Street Journal*. August 18, 1999 (p. A1).

4. Iridium was revived in December 2000 when a group of investors paid $25 million for its assets and repositioned it as a lower cost, specialty provider of global communications for military and commercial applications. In contrast to Motorola's previous multiyear, multibillion-dollar contract to operate Iridium's satellite network, a revamped and slimmed-down Iridium Satellite signed a new operating agreement with Boeing, with monthly operating costs less than 10 percent of the previous contract.

5. Lee Gomes. "Linux Companies Turn to a 'Dot-Com' Pitch to Sidestep Hitch That the Software Is Free." *The Wall Street Journal*. November 8, 1999.

Chapter 5

1. "Why an acquisition? Often, it's the people," Bernard Wysocki. *The Wall Street Journal*. October 6, 1997.

2. Thomas Zizzo. "The high cost of optical networking talent." *Electronic Business*. September 2000; Julie Creswell. "Cold Front." *Fortune*. February 5, 2001.

3. Henry Goldblatt. "Cisco's secrets." *Fortune*. November 8, 1999.

4. Siara and Cerent had more in common than just their astronomical deal valuations. Both companies had been split out of what had been Fiberlane Communications, founded in part by Kleiner Perkins venture capital partner Vinod Khosla, just a couple years earlier. Cyras, another optical-networking company, also emerged out of Fiberlane, but by the time Ciena acquired it in December 2000, the optical market had started to droop and it could fetch "only" $2 billion.

5. Creswell. ibid.

6. Zizzo. ibid.

7. Ed Michaels, Helen Handfield-Jones, and Beth Axelrod. *The War for Talent*. 2001.

8. Ben Elgin. "A Do-It-Yourself Plan at Cisco: No more reliance on acquisitions." *Business Week*. September 10, 2001.

9. Goodwill is the difference between the price an acquirer pays for an acquisition and the fair book value of the acquired company's net assets. A price premium above net-asset value represents "goodwill," a catch-all term meant to capture the difficult-to-measure, intangible worth of an acquired company. Historically, under U.S. accounting standards, the cost of this M&A goodwill usually was amortized and written off over a period of up to 40 years. Under new accounting rules pushed by the U.S. SEC and taking effect at the end of 2001, goodwill no longer had to be amortized. Instead, it was simply to be carried forward on the books of the acquirer as

an intangible asset. If the goodwill became "impaired," however—of lower value than that recorded on the books— companies had to recognize this and reflect the impairment by taking a one-time accounting charge (loss).

10. Chris Sewell. "When boom goes bust." *Telephony*. October 22, 2001.

11. For example, David J. Teece. "Profiting from Technological Innovation: Implications for Integration, Collaboration, Licensing and Public Policy." *Research Policy*. Volume 15, Issue 6. 1996.

12. For example, Gerard J. Tellis and Peter N. Golder. "First to market, first to fail? Real causes of enduring market leadership." *Sloan Management Review*. Volume 37, Issue 2. 1996.

13. Annette L. Ranft and Michael D. Lord. "Acquiring new knowledge: The role of retaining human capital in acquisitions of high-tech firms." *Journal of High Technology Management Research*. Volume 11, Issue 2. 2000.

14. John A. Byrne and Ben Elgin. "Cisco Shopped Till It Nearly Dropped." *Business Week*. January 21, 2002.

15. Ranft and Lord, 2000. ibid.

16. Palm paid just $170 million in stock, or a very modest multiple of only seven-tenths times sales; Handspring's original IPO day close had left it with a market capitalization of $3.4 billion. Of course, by the time of the deal, Palm itself was down to about $300 million in market capitalization, after having peaked ever-so-briefly at more than $90 billion on its own IPO day.

17. Annette L. Ranft and Michael D. Lord. "Acquiring new technologies and capabilities: A grounded model of acquisition implementation." *Organization Science*. July/August 2002.

18. Jeff Walsh and Ed Scannell. "Tivoli-IBM union yields fruit, but integration work remains." *InfoWorld*. March 3, 1997.

Chapter 6

1. For example, Adrian J. Slywotzsky and David J. Morrison. "The Spin-Out Business Design." *The Profit Zone*. 1997.

2. Jeffrey W. Allen. "Capital markets and corporate structure: The equity carve-outs of Thermo Electron." *Journal of Financial Economics*. April 1998.

3. Slywotzsky and Morrison, ibid.

Index

Making Strategy Work

Without effective execution, no business strategy can succeed. Unfortunately, most managers know far more about developing strategy than about executing it—and overcoming the difficult political and organizational obstacles that stand in their way. In this book, Lawrence Hrebiniak offers the first comprehensive, disciplined process model for making strategy work in the real world. Hrebiniak has consulted on execution and strategy with companies ranging from GM to Chase Manhattan, DuPont to GE (where he participated in several of Jack Welch's legendary Work-Outs). Drawing on his unsurpassed experience, Hrebiniak shows why execution is even more important than many senior executives realize, and sheds powerful new light on why businesses fail to deliver on even their most promising strategies.

ISBN 013146745X, © 2005, 408 pp., $27.95

Failsafe Strategies

In the 1990s, in the name of "revolutionary business models," businesses took on massive risks almost without concern. Today, many companies have become powerfully averse to taking the risks that are essential to long-term success. Now, there's a whole new way to think about risk: one that liberates you to act, while protecting you against danger. Dr. Sayan Chatterjee shows how to identify high-risk, high-return opportunities, and then systematically manage and reduce those risks up front, as you design your initiative… not after you operationalize it. Using his techniques, you can safely pursue opportunities your competitors will walk away from—and sustain profit growth far into the future.

ISBN 0131011111, © 2005, 312 pp., $26.95